Lean Semesters

CRITICAL UNIVERSITY STUDIES

Jeffrey J. Williams and Christopher Newfield, Series Editors

Lean Semesters

How Higher Education Reproduces Inequity

Sekile M. Nzinga

 JOHNS HOPKINS UNIVERSITY PRESS   BALTIMORE

© 2020 Johns Hopkins University Press
All rights reserved. Published 2020
Printed in the United States of America on acid-free paper
9 8 7 6 5 4 3 2 1

Johns Hopkins University Press
2715 North Charles Street
Baltimore, Maryland 21218-4363
www.press.jhu.edu

Library of Congress Cataloging-in-Publication Data

Names: Nzinga, Sekile, M. 1971– author.
Title: Lean semesters : how higher education reproduces inequity /
    Sekile M. Nzinga.
Description: Baltimore : Johns Hopkins University Press, [2020] |
    Series: Critical university studies | Includes bibliographical
    references and index.
Identifiers: LCCN 2019057268 | ISBN 9781421438764 (hardcover) |
    ISBN 9781421438771 (ebook)
Subjects: LCSH: African American women college teachers—
    Social conditions. | Minority women college teachers—United
    States—Social conditions. | African American women in higher
    education—Social conditions. | Minority women in higher
    education—United States—Social conditions. | Sex discrimina-
    tion in higher education—United States. | Racism in higher
    education—United States. | Educational equalization—United
    States. | Education, Higher—Social aspects—United States.
Classification: LCC LB2332.32 .N95 2020 | DDC 378.1/2082—dc23
LC record available at https://lccn.loc.gov/2019057268

A catalog record for this book is available from the British Library.

*Special discounts are available for bulk purchases of this book. For more
information, please contact Special Sales at specialsales@press.jhu.edu.*

Johns Hopkins University Press uses environmentally friendly book
materials, including recycled text paper that is composed of at least
30 percent post-consumer waste, whenever possible.

To Black women within and beyond the academy

In memory of Rosalyn Terborg-Penn

Contents

Acknowledgments

This book is both testimony and a solidarity project, one in which I owe deep gratitude to a chorus of people, both inside and outside of higher education. I give priority and the highest gratitude to my study participants and to those Black academic women whose professional, educational, and personal lives have often been reduced to statistical data points as casualties of higher education under neoliberalism. Each of my study participants fueled my persistence to complete this book, and I am deeply grateful for their trust and their fearlessness as they shared their truths. I stand in unbending solidarity with them as they continue to fight for the lives and careers they deserve. I hope they each feel seen, heard, and valued through this work. I also want to thank the contributors to my edited volume, *Laboring Positions*, for inspiring me to interrogate the themes that emerged in that collection in a sustained form. The testimonies and theories put forth by Vanessa Marr, Stacia Brown, Yolanda Covington Ward, and Alexis Pauline Gumbs have informed much of this current project. Additionally, I thank my dear Ivy Beyond the Wall, Rosalyn Terborg-Penn, a pioneering scholar of Black women's history who passed away during the writing of this book. She was the undergrad professor whose class I never took while I was a student at Morgan State but whose determined and prolific career has had a tremendous influence on me as a writer and academic-mother.

I also want to thank Greg Britton, editorial director of Johns Hopkins University Press, and Jeffrey Williams, coeditor of JHUP's Critical University Studies series, for their unending patience with this project and for supporting me throughout my often disrupted and derailed writing process. I thank the Gender and Women's Studies Program and the Institute for Race, Research, and Public Policy at the University of Illinois at Chicago (UIC) for their funding during the early research and writing portions of this project. I am also grateful to Northwestern University's Office of the Provost, Office of Institutional Diversity, and Inclusion and Women's Center for supporting me during the final writing phases. I truly appreciate these forms of institutional and financial support, but many marginalized and underrepresented scholars like myself also benefit from a vast array of other informal and formal supports that are often undervalued, underacknowledged, and made invisible by traditional markers of academic labor but deserve inclusion herein.

My dedicated developmental editor, Kim Greenwell, provided me with ongoing feedback as well as the unwavering support that so many of my deserving peers are lacking in the current intensified rat race of academe. Words cannot express how much I appreciated her nonjudgmental counsel as I considered leaving and then left my beloved academic career as well as when I contemplated walking away from this book project in the aftermath of that career-altering decision. Similarly, my sister-mentors Julia Jordan Zachary, Michelle Boyd (Inkwell Writing Retreats), and Nadine Naber deserve all the praise and recognition for possessing the feminist values and intentional practices that help to retain Black women and other women of color scholars in academia. Each of them coaxed and convinced me to keep going and to claim my purpose beyond ever-changing goalposts and the institutionalized devaluations of my intellectual and professional contributions. Additionally, I am eternally grateful to my UIC colleagues Marisha Humphries and Lorena Garcia for welcoming me into their weekly write-on-site sessions and into their supportive community of mother-scholars and scholars of color. I am also grateful to a wide circle of Black feminist sister-scholars who demanded that we write Black women's narratives of resistance and survival, including my own—Lakeesha Harris, Elizabeth Todd Breland, Olivia Perlow, Teri Platt, Camille Wilson, Ruth Nicole Brown, Nikol Alexander Floyd, Adrienne Dixson, Tay Glover, Tokeya Graham, and so many others; I thank you and I affirm you. Thanks, too, to feminist colleagues such as Gwendolyn Beethum, Julianne Guillard, and the members of the National Women's Studies Association's Contingent Labor Interest Group, who are committed to working-class struggles and who take brave stances as they interrogate academic feminism under neoliberalism. I thank academic labor activist and union organizer, Kira Schuman, for her profound solidarity with this project, whether she was assisting me in mapping the current landscape of the academic labor movement or donating her home to me as my writing retreat space.

I would be remiss without thanking my deep and wide circle of friends and family who cared for me and reminded me of who I am throughout this process. I am truly blessed by the fact that there are too many of you to name here, but know that I highly value each of you. Finally, to my partner, Cedric, and my children, Kimathi, Cabral, and Zora, each of you continually inspire me with your brilliance. I deeply appreciate your endless supply of love and affirmation, whether I was stumbling or steeling my way through this project.

The University as Hyper-Producer of Inequity

I search the classifieds for weekend temp jobs that could accommodate my current teaching schedule. Sometimes I don't make a lunch during the lean semesters so the kids have more to eat. If they call during class tonight complaining of hunger, I will stop by the grocery store and use my state-issued $1.25 to pick up something for them to snack on before bedtime.

—Vanessa Marr, graduate student and adjunct professor

Narratives like Vanessa Marr's, a queer Black woman, doctoral student, adjunct faculty member, and parent navigating poverty, are lesser known narratives of academic life, yet they offer a richly layered exposé of the corporatized university and the practices it shares with the US economy under neoliberalism. We are also witnessing graduate students across the country from Columbia to University of Chicago mobilizing against the simultaneous declining quality of their education, its steadily rising costs, the accompanying burden of educational debt, and their own struggles with labor exploitation.

Prior to becoming an academic, I was a social worker. I naively spent most of my early career encouraging Black women who were navigating poverty to stay in school, return to school, or attend college so that they would be better positioned to transcend their social location. Fast-forward 25 years, and many of my highly educated and accomplished academic colleagues' material conditions look eerily similar to my former clients' realities. As a tenure-track academic occupying a location of "outsider within" (Collins 1986), I began writing this book to map the lived impact of neoliberalism and to name the opaque ways in which the market practices of contemporary higher education institutions are compounding inequity for Black women in the twenty-first century.

I did so while being fully cognizant that Black women are indeed graduating with advanced degrees more than ever before. Yet the corporatized university, long celebrated as a purveyor of progress and opportunity, is systematically and en masse indebting Black women then disposing of their bodies and their intellectual contributions, as well as their potential. In addition, Black women's motivations toward achievement have often been packaged to figure centrally in higher education institutions' marketing campaigns, which deliver messages that these are institutions that educate and provide opportunity to all, regardless of their social and economic position. In fact, however, more and more college-educated and accomplished Black women, including my fellow colleagues like Vanessa Marr, face strained and worsening economic, material, and labor conditions—ones that are similar to those endured by my former clients who aspired to attend college. Though I remain committed to the liberating, democratizing, and economic potential of higher education and intellectual careers, these institutional paradoxes require sustained analysis by women of color feminists on the impact of the unjust and discriminatory practices of contemporary higher education institutions.

My central argument is that, far from being a site generative of equality and opportunity, the university—whether private, for-profit, or not-for-profit—currently operates as a *hyper-producer of inequity* for marginalized populations, particularly academic women of color. Furthermore, in light of the corporatization of academic labor, the privatization of education, and other critical shifts in higher education, such dynamics must be recognized as *intrinsic*, not tangential, to the operation of the neoliberal university. The volume draws upon the work of Black academic women,[1] feminists, and other scholars critical of the university[2] who have collectively interrogated the various forms of inequity produced and reproduced by higher education institutions. It also contributes to both feminist and critical university studies perspectives by addressing lacunae within their respective analyses.

Academic feminists and women of color have been some of the first to raise concerns regarding the rise of contingent academic labor. They have long offered important gender perspectives to the uneven distribution of part-time faculty appointments, noting that women were more likely to land these positions instead of tenure-track appointments. Eileen Schell (1998) exposed the burgeoning field of writing instruction in the 1990s and documented the failures of professionalism. Schell's critical study also revealed institutionalized sexism via the disproportionate hiring of women as contingent writing instructors. Black women are disproportionately hired in nontenure-track positions across academic fields, but even within this process they are often overlooked or not sought after during a hiring process that relies heavily, if informally, on professional networks of white faculty to which these women are often not privy. At the same time, though they may only be hired as part-time and possibly teach only one course per year, their demographic data is included by colleges and universities in diversity counts. The present study takes these academic hiring practices into consideration and extends prior gender-only analyses by examining how even the contingent labor market unduly penalizes Black women in nuanced ways.

While the modern academic labor movement has gained momentum, it seems that many volumes of testimonials, published research, and professional conferences concerning the institutionalized barriers facing academic women of color have been omitted from the dominant articulations of the current crises in higher education. For example, Tressie Mc-Millan Cottom's 2017 groundbreaking exposé of for-profit institutions exemplifies the need to also map the economic and material conditions of women of color that are being produced and reproduced by the current political economy of the corporatized and privatized university. With this volume, I hope to offer a necessary addition to women of color studies critical of the university, with a central focus on the university as a contributor to Black academic women's educational, professional, and economic inequity.

As such, the book contributes to the growing critical discourse on the neoliberalization and corporatization of higher education and its crippling impact on the university, its cultural productions, and the citizenry within and beyond its boundaries. I consider how intersecting hierarchies of gender and race are fortified by the market forces that are currently restructuring US colleges and universities, which are taking a devastating professional and economic toll on Black women academics' lives and careers. By foregrounding the racialized and gendered practices of the university, I also offer a sustained intervention by a feminist woman of color into the singularity of class-based analyses focused on the negative effects of neoliberal policies but inattentive to their unequal distribution.

By emphasizing racial and economic inequity in my feminist analysis, I also offer a much-needed extension of previous gender-only analyses that have been dominant within the discourse on institutionalized barriers faced by academic women yet that remain silent on structural racism and the role of economic stratification within the context of higher education. This book highlights the ways in which past liberal feminist "victories" within academia have yet to become accessible to all women, especially to those whose lives and experiences both within and beyond academia are complicated by labor exploitation and discriminatory treatment mired in gendered racism.

An Unmarked Site for Hyper-Production of Inequity

Black women have historically borne the brunt of inequitable US social policies and continue to be one of the most socially and economically vulnerable groups in the United States. In the early twenty-first century, they are living through an era of austerity and are experiencing a disproportionate impact of the Great Recession of 2008. In addition, the Trump administration's erratic and conservative social, educational, and labor policy decisions are having a lopsided, negative impact on Black women's livelihoods. The unemployment rate for Black women was 6.5 percent in July 2017, the lowest it had been in over a decade prior to and since the Great Recession. However, Black women's unemployment rate is still nearly twice that of white men, and data suggest that they are recovering more slowly since the 2008 Great Recession than other groups (Temple 2017). In addition, men's wages have risen while women's have remained stagnant between 2000 and 2018. The gender wage gap for young college graduates has also widened over the past 18 years, growing from 11 percent to 14.7 percent. Because Black women face racial disparities in pay in addition to the gender pay gap, Black women workers' wages suffered steep declines in the 2008 Great Recession and its aftermath. In addition, young Black college graduates continue to be underemployed and face a 16.8 percent wage penalty relative to their white counterparts (Gould, Mokhiber, & Wolfe 2018). These compounded labor disparities translate into lower wages and significantly larger salary penalties for Black women.

Despite, and possibly in response to, the current unfruitful economic climate, Black women in the United States have seen a marked increase in college and graduate school participation over the past 30 years. The defunding and privatization of higher education has resulted in fewer comprehensive financial aid packages being awarded, so their achievements are tempered by the often crushing educational and consumer debt they accrue along the way. For those who attend graduate school with a desire to become professors, the lack of tenure-track appointments to which they have access upon graduation and the educational and consumer debt they carry into their careers contribute to their already deepening professional and economic disadvantage.

Scholars critical of the practices of the university have long since exposed its market logic and prevailing ideologies of labor exploitation, yet universities have often positioned themselves as victims, suggesting that they are simply responding to the massive defunding of higher education. Many assume that tuition hikes are a necessary evil to keep colleges and universities operational, but during the same time period, we have witnessed the number of college administrators grow and their salaries balloon while the ranks and rights of full-time tenure-track faculty dwindled. The rise of the managerial class in academia is a key indicator that the university is no longer centrally committed to educating students and employing intellectual workers but instead is concerned with managing bodies and profiting from a corporatized knowledge economy (Ross 2012).

Higher education institutions are not the only sector impacted by neoliberal decision making. The rapidly advancing neoliberal political economy in the United States has severely assaulted all social institutions, which has taken a toll on its most vulnerable populations. Thus, increased privatization of child and elder care as well as health and mental health care has placed significant strain on families and communities to extend their informal caregiving of loved ones. These retrenchments have increased Black women's caretaker burden and continue to compromise their livelihoods (Chang 2010). These complex social and economic conditions, exacerbated outside the academy, also threaten Black women and working-class women and the promise of their intellectual work within the academy. This particularly is the case for Black women graduate students, staff, and faculty members who are caring for others within their families and who are also committed to demanding justice for vulnerable communities. In addition, the academy's boundless work demands, its assumption of an infinite availability of adjunct and part-time faculty, its waning job security, and its prizing of institutional profit over collective gain intensifies the career vulnerability of Black women and other women of color academics and risks straining faculty members' connections in their familial and community lives, as well as their personal well-being.

Women of Color's Feminist Critique of Higher Education

This study considers the multiple ways in which the contemporary university intensifies and is producing new forms of inequity for underrepresented women of color by drawing upon national data and the deeply insightful narratives of Black academic women themselves. The volume focuses on four pressure points within higher education: the graduate school process, faculty appointments, parenting and caregiving as academic women, and attrition. In addition, the fourth chapter foregrounds the embodied theories of Black women academics who offer both institutional analyses and a blueprint toward the imagined futures of higher education.

The book also expands contemporary analyses of the university as an institution and a site of intellectual inquiry. Most studies tend to examine one location along the academic trajectory, but I look at the experiences of both graduate student women and faculty women as I map "graduate school–to–food stamps pathways" fueled by the privatization of higher education and the casualization of academic labor. My economic analysis of the impact of educational debt and its enduring implications beyond graduate school makes clear that Black women academics are hardly allowed to demarcate between the phases of their academic lives. In addition, by examining the multiplicity of "affective labor," which is disproportionately performed by women of color faculty, staff, and graduate students on and off campus, I expand the necessary scope of critical university studies by deploying a woman of color feminist perspective in highlighting how the university interfaces with the professional and private lives of Black academic women. One of the most powerful challenges to the protected and projected image of academia is the proliferation of ways in which the effects of its privatized practices have begun to detrimentally penetrate beyond one's career.

I draw upon both extensive interview data and a wide range of national reports on the economic and material conditions of three of the most vulnerable groups of academics: Black women graduate students, Black women contingent faculty, and Black women academic caregivers. I utilize several national data sources to support my claims (e.g., the American Association of University Professors, the American Federation of Teachers, the Center for American Progress, the US Department of Education's National Center for Education Statistics, the US Department of Education's Integrated Postsecondary Education Data System, and the American Institutes for Research). These large-scale data and reports expose the alarming disjuncture between the increase in women of color obtaining PhDs, the extent of their debt accrual, and the subsequent career stall experienced by those who attempt to enter the academic labor market. They also document the growing predominance of non-tenure-track faculty in America's colleges and universities and the lack of tenure-track faculty opportunities.

The voices of Black graduate students and faculty themselves are central to my theorizations. In 2013 and 2014, I conducted a series of semiformal interviews with 31 women at various stages of their academic careers, including some who had made the painful decision to leave the very system in which they had invested so much of their time, resources, money, and intellectual energy. Although I do not disclose the full specificity of their identities or scholarly interests,[3] these precariously situated academic women had expertise in a wide variety of fields and were most often trained and published within the professions, social sciences, humanities, and/or interdisciplinary fields. Collectively, they had between 2 and 10 years of college teaching experience as non-tenure-track faculty at the time that I interviewed them. Most had acquired their doctorate degree, a few were in the final stages of their doctoral education, and one participant had a terminal master's degree. They taught at institutions ranging from community colleges to major research universities. Most participants taught at colleges and universities in the southeastern states, while others taught at schools in the Midwest and mid-Atlantic regions. Two had been active in faculty unions, but the majority worked at institutions with no collective bargaining units. One participant held a full-time, non-tenure-track, multiyear position, but all of the other interviewees secured their teaching positions on a semester-to-semester basis. Some had teaching appointments within one institution, while others traveled between two or more institutions. Some participants supplemented their academic income with jobs outside of higher education, while others received financial support from their domestic partners, family members, and/or through public assistance. Their incomes from ranged from $7,800 to $40,000 annually. Those with higher annual household incomes benefited from their partners' income. All but one participant were parents/caregivers, and the vast majority had live-in dependent children and/or adult dependents. Only two participants had employer-based health insurance, while others had state-sponsored health insurance, community-based reduced fee health care, or were considered dependents on the spouse's or child's father's insurance plan.

Over a third of the participants requested that they not be directly quoted, fearing that they would be exposed given the low number of Black academic women working and studying in higher education, while one participant requested that I use her real name in order to establish a historical record of her position on the contemporary politics of higher education. Those self-determined preferences notwithstanding, their collective testimonies, storytelling, and interpretations of their experiences serve as a compelling intervention and witnessing project in the discourse surrounding the corporatized university and help to raise the critical consciousness necessary to respond to broader social inequities and institutionalized injustices.

As these women are experts on their own lives and are acutely aware of the exploitation and discrimination they experienced, I serve primarily as an interlocutor with a shared purpose: to interrogate the contemporary university as an unmarked site of their marginalization. The analytical lens I use to frame their narratives, as well as the national data, is an intersectional feminist one that recognizes the multiplicity of not only people's identities and experiences but also institutionalized hierarchies of power, such as race and gender, as well as stratified and segmented labor structures. The grounded theory that I both draw on and produce thus starts with Black women's lived experiences as precarious graduate students and academic workers and seeks to explain those experiences by embedding them within the contemporary and historical contexts that shape *and* delimit them. The book's unique combination of national data, policy analysis, and compelling testimony provides a powerful nexus that invites its readers to reconsider popular conceptions of the university as a no-fault monument of equal opportunity. My method of foregrounding Black women's educational and work narratives within the book was a critical decision that honored the methods of life history. Leith Mullings suggests that

> what ideally marks Black feminist research is its grounding in the unique interaction of race, class, and gender from which emerges the experiences of African American women and its rootedness in communities of resistance. The enterprise is both descriptive in writing African American women into history and corrective in its critique of male dominated, patriarchal social theories and interpretations of women's lives that may be functions of class, race and gender hierarchies. (2000, 27)

In addition, I intend for this study to serve as a "witnessing" project of the type described by labor studies scholar Jack Metzger:

> Think of it as workers *witnessing* their own plight, calling for others in similar situations to join them and appealing to those of us with decent incomes to support them. Witnessing, with its religious overtones, is not intended as an immediately practical action. It's first about individuals summoning the courage to put

themselves forward to make a public claim that they are one of thousands (millions nationally) who are being treated unjustly. In this case, it means taking the risk that they may be fired or otherwise disciplined for leaving work and going into the streets to proclaim, "We are worth more." Witnessing is meant to make us think about justice as the witnesses simultaneously inspire and shame us with the courage of their individual actions. (2013, 1)

The narratives and national data within this book situate contemporary academic life within the broader context of the privatization and corporatization of higher education, but they also challenge characterizations of that context as a relatively recent invention that affects all academics unilaterally. This work reveals that neoliberalism's economic and social stronghold on higher education is not evenly distributed but is racialized and gendered, which disproportionately impacts underrepresented women of color. It also historicizes these developments by emphasizing, crucially, that the marginalization of women of color by and within academia is neither new nor adequately recognized in contemporary academic labor struggles. Its analysis ultimately informs us of the structural inequities encapsulated within and often hidden from our sight by the resilient enshrinement of the university as a fundamentally progressive institution. Such is the distorted imagery that simultaneously renders the experiences of women of color within academia invisible and undervalued but then appropriates their hard-fought success stories as marketing tools to demonstrate the university's purported achievement of access, choice, and equity.

Structural Overview

Each chapter uniquely maps the current threats of corporatization and privatization within higher education and creates space for Black academic women to narrate their experiences and subversive modes of resistance and survival under such conditions. In doing so, I hope to offer a level of methodological and analytical sophistication that is essential to unpack the university's function not just as an institution that is failing in its democratizing potential but as one that is operating as a hyper-producer of inequity for Black academic women.

In chapter 1, "Mortgaging Our Brains," I note how academic institutions structurally reproduce inequity by pricing out Black women, who are less likely to be able to afford a college education, particularly a graduate education. I chart the targeting of Black women students and other underrepresented students of color by private financial institutions that entice students with unregulated and unsubsidized student loans at higher rates. Black women—the least likely group to be funded by their institutions for their graduate education and, in turn, the most likely to fund their education privately—face the highest educational loan debt at both the undergraduate and graduate level of any group in the nation. The burden of educational debt is often met with a dire job market both inside and outside of the university and is producing what I refer to as a "graduate school–to–food stamps pipeline." A growing number of women and people of color struggle to traverse this reality, only to emerge on the other side with none of the social and economic benefits that were expected to materialize as a result of their educational accomplishments. These complex economic burdens, produced by governmental disinvestment, corporate greed, and institutional complicity are only amplified by the well-documented racial and gender barriers of inadequate mentorship by overburdened faculty and the hostile professional climate that women of color must navigate.

In chapter 2, "Ain't I Precarious?," I turn to the overrepresentation of women of color faculty, particularly Black women, as contingent laborers within the increasingly segmented, feminized, and racialized academic workforce. I argue that Black women experience an intensified form of precariousness as academic laborers who are both *contractually* and *structurally* contingent. Faculty of color, particularly women of color, are contractually contingent under the university's latest restructured formation—a position shared by a growing majority of university faculty who are similarly subject to an increasingly corporatized and precarious workplace, but also a position within which women of color are disproportionately represented and impacted. Compounding this circumstance, and their official appointment status notwithstanding, Black women academics are also *structurally* contingent. By that I am suggesting that tenure-track Black women remain contingent because of institutionalized forms of racism and sexism that systematically bypass them in hiring and devalue their labor and contributions by disposing of them during tenure and promotion processes. Contractual and structural forms of contingency, both of which Black women and other underrepresented women of color face and have historically identified as their joint sites of struggle, have not been acknowledged by current iterations of the academic labor movement. In some instances, these long-articulated labor struggles have even been obscured and exacerbated by contemporary labor discourse that deploys racialized and gendered frames to animate the mainstream adjunct teaching crisis with little stated commitment to racially marginalized and structurally contingent faculty members.

In chapter 3, "Families Devalued," I challenge the corporatized university's professed diversity rhetoric and gender equality commitments ostensibly enacted through its "family friendly" and "inclusive" institutional policies and practices. We see here the limits of liberal feminists' focus on "gender equity," exclusive of racial and economic justice. Women of color historically face greater caregiver burdens, have significant family and community responsibilities, and are more vulnerable to educational and career disruption given the lack of institutional support for working women with families. Graduate students as well as contingent, tenure-track, and tenured Black academic women alike must navigate the precariousness of their academic positions in terms of the racialized and gendered readings of their reproduction, competence, and work ethic. Furthermore, narrowly conceived "gender equality" policies reinforce heteronormativity and capitalist notions of individualism, along with the intensification of work. This chapter demonstrates the ways that Black women are less likely to benefit from family leave policies and are more likely to rely on personal resources or support from the state owing to the economic barriers they must navigate. Their narratives reveal that for contractually contingent Black academic women to be able to continue to "do what they love," they are subject to relying on their spouses, their children's fathers, or the state. These conditions reproduce forms of racial, economic, and gender inequity as Black women who strive to be autonomous intellectual workers instead risk reproducing heteronormative dependency. This chapter wrestles with the interplay between disenfranchisement and empowerment, but most notably the stories herein provide an intimate window onto the tenacity of institutionalized inequity for women of color in the United States.

Finally, whereas the other chapters of the book document the institutionalized and market-driven barriers confronting highly educated, professionally committed Black women who struggle, scrape by, and persist, chapter 4, "Jumping Mountains," showcases the narratives of Black academic women who, in spite of these conditions, offer us a blueprint for salvaging the university as a democratizing social institution.

The theorizations in this chapter reveal that Black women are not only creatively confronting the hand they have been dealt but are teaching, publishing, leading, and subversively transforming society both within and beyond the walls of colleges and universities. As Wanda Evans-Brewer noted, they are indeed "jumping mountains" and choosing to operate outside the imposed, market-driven boundaries of the privatized and corporatized university. In many ways their exemplary academic work and situated analyses point us back toward a place and space of educational justice as they construct intellectual "homeplaces," accessible pedagogies, transformative curricula, and social discourse or justice on and off campus.

Ultimately, this book is a testimony and witnessing project. Laura Nixon argues that "when advocates put the needs of the most marginalized people at the center of their theorizing and strategic plan, it is more likely that everyone's needs will ultimately be met" (2013, 100). It urgently asserts that centering the experiences of Black women is a critical starting point for reclaiming higher education as a social good for all.

Chapter One

Mortgaging Our Brains: Black Women, Privatization, and Subprime PhDs

Getting a PhD is not cheap. Sometimes I'm in a panic about it, sometimes not. I look at it like a second mortgage. [*Laughs.*] I mortgaged my brain!

—Charli, PhD candidate and adjunct

In the spring of 2014, I participated in a panel on the neoliberal university at the Freedom Dreams, Freedom Now conference at University of Illinois at Chicago. Delighted to be included in the program, I focused my comments on the recent academic labor unionization victories at UIC and how tenure-track faculty must persist by connecting with broader struggles to reclaim public education. I offered a few introductory comments on the need to align academic labor struggles with students' struggles for educational justice. I spoke of the disproportionate impact of university privatization on students of color and mentioned how a sense of shame surrounding student debt prevented broader discussion of the material and economic costs of college education in this historical moment. The steep cost of a college education and the burden of student loan debt were central to my comments concerning the need for faculty to join students in collectivizing and mobilizing around educational justice. Not one person in the audience asked me a question or engaged the issues I had raised during the open discussion that followed. I sat wondering if I had missed the mark in the five minutes I was allotted and considered whether my comments were out of line topically and/or politically with those of my esteemed co-panelists. Were my comments not relevant to my audience of primarily student and faculty activists of color?

Interestingly, after the panel ended some Black women immediately approached me from the audience. One was in tears as she approached. The women, both with doctoral degrees, thanked me for speaking to their struggles and naming them out loud. They expressed feelings of pain, guilt, shame, confusion, and betrayal. It was then that the magnitude of the moment hit me. The loud silence that I observed was produced out of the privatized and individualized shame that I had referenced in my comments. I also understood more fully why my comments may not have been publicly discussed. After all, how could someone safely "expose" oneself as economically struggling when one was supposed to be a successful academic, a committed activist, and a model community member? How dare someone break the silence and disclose the economic penalties and subsequent traumas of an advanced and highly coveted education? How could students and faculty members from underrepresented groups give themselves permission to acknowledge economic hardships when they are constantly reminded of the opportunities unavailable to previous generations or even others in their families and communities? How could the Black women who approached me expose the struggles related to the exceedingly high costs of their education and their need for economic support without evoking the racialized and gendered stereotype of the state-dependent "welfare queen"? Conversely, what ideologies and institutional practices produce these conditions within higher education and its aftermath in the twenty-first century? Most important, how do contemporary Black women in academia, in spite of the above circumstances, make meaning out of their educational journeys and professional aspirations?

These are the questions that ran through my mind that day and that animate both this chapter and, indeed, the larger book project. I highlight them here because they stand in stark contrast to a different set of questions that tend to frame mainstream discussions of higher education—questions that are indisputably important yet limited in their ability to reveal the contemporary impact of privatization and academic restructuring. Who has access to higher education has become a spurious question. Rather, we should ask: To what extent and in what ways are women, people of color, and other underrepresented groups economically exploited by the practices embedded within a twenty-first-century college education? What does college acceptance, increasing enrollment, and degree completion really mean for underresourced and underrepresented women of color, particularly those pursuing an advanced education?

My point here is not to argue that statistics concerning access, enrollment, and other typically reported "signs of progress" are in any way irrelevant; to the contrary, they are a vital part of the story I seek to examine with this book. The problem is that these numbers-focused questions are inherently limited, blinkered by their narrow focus on a particular set of circumstances that are not unlike the top portion of an iceberg—visible for all to see, but dangerously excluding lived portions of Black academic women's experience. Popularized rhetoric about "diversity and inclusion," "completion," and "climate," I argue, tends to dominate discussions of higher education and questions of its accessibility. In doing so, it overshadows another set of questions that are more troubling, in part precisely because they tend to be overlooked, and in part because they tend to be rooted in deeply entrenched structures of inequality. Here I refer to the kinds of questions I posed above, regarding the financial toll and material consequences disproportionately imposed on students and faculty whose struggle is no longer about simply getting *into* academia, but how to *survive* once they have entered and how to be unencumbered when they exit. I refer here to questions that move us beyond the front door of access and into the murky back rooms of affordability; questions that ask not just how many people are graduating, but *at what cost* and *with what prospects*? I raise questions here, too, about what exactly we mean by the "chilly climate" in higher education, which generally has referred to the sexist and misogynist culture that women faculty and students often must traverse. Notions of a hostile working and learning climate must also include who does and does not receive funding, what it is like to have to work a second job, or to have to navigate welfare systems while trying to write a dissertation with limited resources and less institutional support. How do underresourced and cash-strapped students find their way through the often conflicting demands of academic and state institutions? These are the terrains that are not named but that more fully represent the current graduate school landscape for many.

This chapter explores the disjuncture and the silence separating these two sets of questions. It begins by outlining the seeming paradox they present: the growing number of women of color enrolling in and graduating from higher education, and their simultaneous overrepresentation among the students least likely to actually benefit materially from a graduate education. Mapping the enrollment surge of underrepresented groups along with the material and economic after-effects on underrepresented women of color is a matter that deserves further exploration given higher education's stated mission of creating a democratizing society. Drawing upon interviews and published educational narratives, this chapter highlights the complex economic penalties that Black women pay from the moment they gain entry into the university as graduate students and how their social and economic positions are actually maintained and reproduced within an increasingly privatized higher education context. I buttress my interview records with national data that corroborate the multilayered costs of daring to be achievement-oriented and that also reveal academic institutions' business partnerships with the private financial sector, which disproportionately target students of color with unregulated high-interest-rate loans. While acknowledging the continued relevance of questions about access, completion, and climate, the chapter brings into view the other barriers intensifying the already documented forms of exclusion and dominance that limit Black women's success within academia and society at large.

The academic women's stories captured herein offer us insights into their motivations, the roadblocks to their success, and how they are navigating the university in the twenty-first century as aspiring and determined graduate students. Throughout, I draw on my interviews with three overlapping but distinct groups of Black women: those who have earned their master's degree but were deeply interested in pursuing their doctorates, those who were enrolled in doctoral programs, and those who have recently completed their PhDs. The majority of the women in this study were also teaching as contingent faculty members at a wide range of colleges and universities across the United States. Their experiences share much in common with many other US graduate students, but they also reveal the intersecting effects of race, class, and gender oppression that are often omitted from contemporary critical analyses of the university.

The Paradox of Black Women and Higher Education in the United States

Historically, Black women represent some of the lowest wageworkers in the United States and have been disproportionately impacted by the recent massive cuts to public sector jobs as a result of austerity measures.[1] They continue to be greatly impacted by the dwindling social safety nets due to welfare reform.[2] US Black women and their families have also been greatly affected by the 2008 housing market collapse[3] and continue to face housing insecurity given their disproportionate eviction rate.[4] Consequently, US Black women remain largely responsible for navigating the resultant increases in family and community demands, which are born out of these intertwined social, economic, and political factors (Maddix & Sawyer 2013; Nzinga-Johnson 2013). These intertwined dynamics intensify Black women's long-standing economic disadvantage in US society as they simultaneously navigate the skyrocketing costs of higher education, face a stagnant and precarious job market, and are met with structural inequity owing to employment-based racial and gender discrimination.[5] Despite these broader forces at play, Black women are graduating from undergraduate institutions at higher rates and their participation in graduate education is also on the rise.[6]

Though there is notable promise in the fact that Black women in the United States are progressing educationally and professionally, a closer examination of these often overstated trends suggests that Black women remain underrepresented in all levels of education overall and are the most likely group to incur economic penalty rather than prosperity as a result of their efforts to seek advanced education. Understanding this paradox requires an understanding of the larger political and economic shifts in higher education over the past three decades. Like many US social institutions, postsecondary academic institutions have been steadily transformed into a predominantly private, for-profit enterprise. Beginning with Ronald Reagan's Republican administration and including Barack Obama's Democratic administration, every US president over the past thirty years has sought to balance the federal budget by diverting funds from higher education and simultaneously allowing the deregulation of partnerships between academic institutions and private entities, including banks and financial institutions.[7] The retreat from funding education as a national priority has led to a sharp uptick in the cost of postsecondary education, greatly impacting public academic institutions that had previously been economically accessible. In tandem with federal disinvestment, state and institutional appropriations for college student funding that were historically allocated for students with fewer resources have largely been diverted to merit-based funding streams, which tend to advantage white, male, and middle-class students over underrepresented students.

Interestingly, a key tenet of President Barack Obama's educational platform had been to make college affordable and accessible to all Americans who seek it. During his State of the Union address in January 2015, he passionately stated, "I want to work with this Congress, to make sure Americans already burdened with student loans can reduce their monthly payments, so that student loan debt doesn't derail anyone's dream."[8] And yet, during both of his terms, the Obama administration was criticized by student advocacy groups for primarily advancing educational policies that tend to focus on acquiring, managing, and privatizing educational debt, rather than reducing educational costs by reallocating federal funds back into higher education.[9] His solutions were consistent with a neoliberal ideology that places the costs of education, from kindergarten to college, firmly within a market logic. Consequently, more and more US students and their families are having to fund their college educations by taking on huge amounts of educational and consumer debt; for many, this is simply understood as part of the long-term economic hardship that obtaining a modern college education now presents. Yet, these structural barriers have not only stunted access to college for many Americans but have also transformed the socioeconomic potential of receiving a college education for those with limited resources and opportunity once they do reach the campus doors.

While graduate school attracts a significantly smaller segment of the college student population, the cumulative impact of the costs of a graduate education superimposed on a costly undergraduate education compromises graduate students' socioeconomic potential even further. Funding streams for graduate education differ from those available for undergraduates in that there is little federal or state funding available in the form of grants, such as the Pell Grant. Thus, when graduate school hopefuls search for funding, they are met with the inherent financial barriers presented to those with less wealth, particularly students of color who are disproportionately first-generation college attendees and/or from working-class, underresourced families. Additionally, graduate education simply costs more and generally takes longer to complete than an undergraduate degree. The present debt-based era in higher education marks a new social contract with American students, one that has been dubbed the "plastic age" or "debt for degree" era of higher education (Williams 2014, 45). Thus, the true economic costs of higher education, including graduate education, are yet to be calculated.

Yet even with unprecedented rising costs for graduate study, there continues to be a surge in underrepresented women of color enrolling in doctoral programs. Black women's PhD enrollment has doubled in the past 20 years. This steady increase is occurring despite the decline in academic institutions' ability to adequately fund or hire newly minted PhDs as tenure-track professors given the current widespread depletion in tenure-track faculty in US universities and colleges. In addition, even as Black women are obtaining PhDs at higher rates, they also are the least likely to be funded for their doctoral education across fields of study, and coincidentally, as a group they also have been reported to carry the greatest educational debt of any subgroup of doctoral students (Zeiser, Kirshstein, & Tanenbaum 2013). While remaining critical of higher education, Vivyan Adair and Sandra Dahlberg agree that it "provides the means for many women to secure economic solvency and intellectual fulfillment. It offers hope" (2003, 5). Yet for Black women graduate students, it seems that virtues like hope and persistence come with significant price tags and unfulfilled promissory notes for progress.

By questioning the notion of progress, I do not mean to diminish the documented achievements that Black women academics have obtained from higher education nor the contributions they have made. Instead, I aim to expose the practices of privatizing higher education that threaten their potential. Nor do I intend to position Black women as mere victims of this process, devoid of agency; as will eventually become clear, the narratives that Black women scholars offer capture both their creative genius and their resistance in spite of the difficulty of their circumstances. The point is that understanding the structure and function of the modern university requires a wider lens to fully examine its purpose in the United States and its impact on particular groups in this social, political, and economic moment.

Black Women's Motivations and Persistence

This seeming paradox between Black women's increased entry into the higher education system and its failure on so many fronts to facilitate their success begs the question of why they bother: What factors push and pull Black women to strive for achievement within a system that seems so set upon making them pay—literally—for the contributions they make to it? Many people from marginalized communities are motivated by the emancipatory and democratizing potential of education. As I have argued previously, becoming an academic is defined as an act of resistance against a system that has yet to accept their intellectual capabilities. The respondents' personification of the Black woman academic defies both the popularized, inferentially racist representations of the incapable "Black woman" or the unintelligent "other." Neither of these representations is accorded a rightful place in the academy (Nzinga-Johnson 2013). Additionally, obtaining a college education has also historically been linked to one's economic mobility; but perhaps even more important, freedom, respect, and legitimacy have been critical motivations for underrepresented groups. Access to education, particularly higher education, was at the forefront of civil rights and feminist activism and has become a key form of cultural capital and a marker of social justice for Blacks in the United States. Cherida, a recent sociology PhD, explained:

> I believe that college and graduate school are incredibly important, particularly for people of color, particularly for women in nontraditional areas. I think that despite how expensive it gets, we need to figure out a way to still get it because it becomes our advantage. One of the things that happens is that we can collect these accomplishments and credentials and while it may not look like it pays off immediately, in the long run it makes us more marketable.

Assumptions about access and marketability are long-standing and hold some truth. Generally, college-educated people earn more than the non-college-educated. However, earnings are severely compromised by debt, which negatively impacts wealth attainment. African Americans do not experience the same social and economic benefits of college degrees compared with whites and are disproportionately under- and unemployed owing to structural racism (DiTomaso 2012). Nonetheless, viewpoints like Cherida's undergird many Black women's persistence and determination to return to college and gain more education. Such women also recognize that adopting a cavalier or indifferent attitude toward higher education is simply not an option for them. Their prospects *without* higher education are even more limited, and they lack the kind of structural, intergenerational safety net enjoyed by others with more privilege and resources. For example, Marquita reflected on an interview she once conducted with a wealthy white businessman. His perspective on the importance of a college education struck her in particular:

> … *this guy [was] saying he wasn't going to send his kids to college, he didn't think college taught kids things. He said, "I think they should just do an overseas internship." He's the 1 percent, he's extremely wealthy, so he could tell his kids that and they'd be fine because they could live on his income, they could live on whatever connections he had.*

Far from being delusional or naive, Black women entering higher education do so with a sense of optimism to be sure, but one tempered by a grim awareness that optimism alone is insufficient to guarantee their futures.

In spite of their precariousness within the privatized environs of twenty-first-century university culture, the Black women enrolled in PhD programs whom I interviewed often spoke of their desire for an advanced education that stood outside of these dominant constructions of simply wanting a "better life" or "higher pay." Yes, they also offered the typical responses of desiring to make their families and communities proud or pursuing a dream career, but the nuances of their motivations are worth noting here. As women from historically marginalized groups, their individual rationales for pursuing an advanced degree ranged from a desire to impact the world on a larger scale through the production of knowledge or through the interventions that bring about social transformation. Still others were motivated by a desire to pursue an education that had been denied to generations before them.

Another central theme that surfaced involved wanting to prove the world wrong about them as Black women. My interviewees spoke repeatedly of needing and wanting to secure the intellectual authority afforded by a PhD. Many sought education as a form of defense against a society that devalued their worth. As Jendayi, an Ivy League–educated PhD, put it, "My intellectual authority is my greatest asset and ability to connect with people." She viewed this form of authority as an "intellectual defense of herself" as a Black woman in US society. Similarly, Annisha, who recently completed a PhD in marriage and therapy, spoke of her desire to be heard by others:

> I think the desire for me was twofold. I wanted to get the highest degree in my field, and I also wanted to be able to talk with authority. I was already a female, I was Black, and I needed people to listen to me when I spoke. The only way I could see that happening was to have the credentials to say I'm allowed to say what I need to say.

However, Jendayi also pointed out the consequences of her having an achievement orientation as a Black woman. She noted that this defense mechanism, developed out of the need to navigate a racialized and gendered society, also has the potential to make her a target for attack by others who feel their power or privilege is threatened. She noted the backlash so often provoked by her display of competence as a Black woman and shared that she faces constant challenge from those seeking to maintain established hierarchies.

For other women, the struggle is against a different kind of regulation and backlash—namely, one contending with the internalized politics of Black respectability (Paisley 2003). As a single mother, Alexis's account of her attempt to thwart her faith community's judgment is particularly revealing. Again, her response stands outside of typical economic framings of career advancement and intellectual development. She named two distinct ways that her pursuit of a doctoral degree was important for her as a Black woman. One motive reflected the oft-cited factor of individual persistence (Bair and Haworth 2006), while another was aligned with her valuation of education as a Black person:

> I started this program when my oldest was starting elementary school and my youngest was still a toddler. I finished in seven years; I can't fathom having taken all this time away from them and not walking away with something. I just could not have done that to them. I think the other piece is the way I was raised. My grandmother only had an eighth-grade education. She pressed the importance of an education.

But Alexis also asserted her hope that an advanced education could serve as a form of protection against others' judgments and attacks that impose heteronormativity on Black women. She candidly shared her desire to subvert racialized and gendered judgment:

> I believe the third thing was a kind of prideful thing. It's a terrible reason to get a PhD, but it was in the back of my head when I started. I had my master's degree when I had my children. And I was a single parent with both of them, never married. And I just felt, especially

through the church I was a member of, um, extremely judged by the fact that, it didn't matter that I was educated, or employed, and taking care of my sons—all that mattered [was] that I was a single Black woman who didn't have a husband who brought these two boys into this world. And so for me, a PhD was saying, "You know what? Just because I did that doesn't make me less than a person." You see that? I . . . I have discipline! I can put in work! So, I hate to say it—that was a part of it, too. It was almost to ease some of the steam that I was getting from being a single parent.

When I asked if her strategy had been successful, her response revealed both pain and wry amusement:

Oh, no, not at all! All they cared about was like: "Oh, you have a PhD?! And that's lovely. When are you getting married?!" If the fact that I don't have a ring on my finger matters more than the fact that I try to be a decent person and I'm tryna' raise my children to be decent people, I can't with you guys, "bye"!

Alexis's personal journey and frustrations reflect just some of the forces that inform Black women's decisions regarding education—decisions that are not always or solely economically motivated. Thus the interconnections between sociocultural resistance, individual desire, intellectual curiosity, and economic necessity shape the historical and contemporary context necessary to understand Black women's entry into higher education and their persistence no matter the costs.

Economically Exploiting Ambition

It is particularly critical for us to understand the pursuit of PhDs by Black women even in the face of economic hardship because contemporary academic institutions have begun to prey upon these identified motivations to attract Black women and exploit their well-documented histories of persistence and resistance. For example, a late-night round of TV surfing will most likely locate advertisements from several for-profit academic institutions such as Everest and the University of Phoenix. These ads regularly rely on Black women actors, often portrayed as mothers, to promote their institutions' accessibility. The commercials typically evoke themes of independence, empowerment, maternalized student-professor relationships, self-reliance, and resilience. Furthermore, given the aforementioned rising costs of the advanced degrees and related financial barriers, Black women are also more likely to apply to such relatively less prestigious but more affordable second-tier institutions, as well as regional and public universities for their doctoral studies. The noted rise in doctoral programs, whether public or private, is increasing despite little investment in the infrastructure to support the students and faculty who populate them. Tressie McMillan Cottom and others have rightfully criticized for-profit academic institutions' targeting of women of color and working-class students through the deployment of themes of independence and empowerment in marketing and recruitment materials (Neem et al. 2012). Alternatively, public institutions have been largely successful in marketing themselves as equal opportunity sites and as progressive and diverse academic spaces, yet such imagery says little about institutions' actual capacity or willingness to support the diverse student body they attract or their affordability. This rise in graduate programs has drawn widespread criticism, and many wonder if the uptick in doctoral program offerings is less concerned with preparing students for academic and professional careers or even to benefit faculty members, but are instead developed to serve as profit generators for academic and financial institutions.[10]

For all too many students, the joy of being accepted into a doctoral program is soon replaced with the angst of securing funding. This reality leads the majority of underresourced Black women to turn to student loans for graduate school. Yet graduate student loan borrowers receive few of the federal protections from interest rate increases that undergraduate subsidized loans receive. For example, in 2012, to save about $1.8 billion a year, Congress halted the subsidization of interest that accumulates on federal student loans taken out by graduate students while they are enrolled in school and for the first six transitional "grace period" months after they complete their degrees or are no longer enrolled. In other words, since 2012, US graduate students have been accumulating interest on their government-sponsored loans beginning on the first day of class. If they take longer to complete their degrees, as Black graduate students are likely to do, then they will accrue even greater educational debt if they are not fully funded recipients of fellowships and assistantships.

These risky financial practices affect all US college students who must pay for their own education, but as in the subprime mortgage crisis of 2007–10, trends of uneven impact for people of color and women have become apparent. And in parallel fashion to the housing debt crisis in the United States, the $1.3 trillion student loan debt crisis that affects all American families is disproportionately impacting students and families of color. However, students of color, now more aptly named borrowers of color, most often require greater financial assistance while in school, and many often leave school, whether they graduate or not, with higher levels of educational and consumer debt and with lower levels of income and wealth. Marquita, a Black woman with a master's degree who has considered pursuing a PhD, candidly described the false choice facing many African Americans when a college education is within sight:

You're not even thinking of it in terms of the costs. You're like okay, if signing this is going to get me into school, I'm signing it. And not thinking "I'm going to be making these payments for the rest of my life." There wasn't savings. There wasn't a college fund and always paycheck to paycheck. I wouldn't really want Sarina [her daughter] to go to college and take on all this debt. There was another adjunct I was teaching with. She had a daughter starting college. She was a single mother. She was teaching like six classes on various campuses. She said people would ask, "How are you sending your daughter to college?" She said, "The same way I went to college! That was loans. There's no other way." She was like, "I told her if she didn't get a scholarship, she was going to have to pick up loans." That's just how it is. We want the kids to go to college, and they have to take on all this debt to get it. It's terrible, but that's how it is.

Affirming Marquita's testimony, a 2012 report on student loan debt revealed that Black students have the highest private student loan participation rate in the country and that approximately 81 percent of Black students currently borrow money, compared to 65 percent of white students. The report suggests that the impact of student debt on borrowers of color is complex, because even when they manage to secure loans, they are often saddled with higher interest rates than white students (Johnson, Van Ostern, & White 2012). Private student lenders have been scrutinized by financial regulators for abusing lending practices, but the Trump administration's education secretary loosened oversight regulations in 2018. Private lenders have been operating, thus far successfully, in a murky legal gray zone and have even found mechanisms to penalize borrowers of color for attending schools that have higher educational loan defaults by using a sophisticated "cohort default rate."[11] In addition, banks and financial institutions often prey on students' economic vulnerability and the disparity experienced outside of their educational circumstances by enticing them with exorbitant loan amounts that exceed their need for direct education expenses.

Not surprisingly, the mounting levels of high interest rates on student loans leave borrowers of color and working-class students struggling to make payments on time, often resulting in unforeseen fees for deferment or forbearance. In turn, students of color have higher attrition, more loan defaults, and more debt at both the undergraduate and graduate level. The long-term material impact on students and their families include garnisheed checks, reduced wages, loss of federal income tax rebates, negative credit ratings, and no federal debt protection through bankruptcy. These compounding factors are now being linked to student borrowers' and their cosigner family members' lowered ability to buy homes, save, invest, and prepare for retirement.

In Jeffrey Williams's (2014) powerful argument for the return of accessible higher education, he exposes the psychological and emotional harm of student debt, which he argues is at crisis levels and represents a breach of the US social contract. His research illuminates student loan borrowers' narratives of the high rates of depression, anxiety, and suicidal ideation engendered by this unprecedented level of privatized burden. These conditions are produced within a political climate of cutbacks in health and human services and limited on-campus mental health services. Charli noted that when she did have to rely on loans for her studies, they were from financial private institutions, which resulted in higher interest rates and harsher penalties during repayment periods. She disclosed the emotional toll imposed by this level of debt:

Okay. Can I say something about those private loans? My husband paid off two private loans, one to Discover, one through Citibank. They were only $1,500 each. When I tell you I was trying to pay them off as hard as I could. I couldn't. My husband says it looked like the interest was compounded daily on one of my loans. Sometimes I'm hard on myself, and I say, "Maybe I shouldn't have taken this loan." There was one time when I refused a particular loan through financial aid. There were times when I refused some financial aid because I didn't think it was needed. But $1,500/class per semester, I needed those loans to live.

Charli also expressed feelings of deep shame and resentment as she made decisions that were critical to her and her family's survival. She timidly asked, "Would you think I was a bad person if I told you I didn't want to calculate how much student loans I have? Let's just say I have over $100,000 total." Her confession and anxiety regarding her mounting debt joins the chorus of other respondents who made similar claims during my conversations with them.

Niyah also disclosed her extreme level of debt when discussing how she shared her premarital financial status with her fiancé.[12] She described telling him, "Look, here's some things you need to know. Number one, number two, number three. I just told my partner about my house full of debt." The term "mortgage" echoed throughout my interviews and exposed patterns of meaning regarding the respondents' awareness of financial institutions' intention to tether them and their families to long-term debt for their degrees. Alexis, a recent PhD, now campus administrator and adjunct faculty member, shared that she too had close to six figures in student loan debt; when I asked how she planned to repay her loan, she replied:

What I did was apply for the income-based repayment plan. The first time I did it, the payment was still too high given my household size and the dynamics, and the fact that I am a single parent who does not receive child support. I called back and I spoke to a lady who mentioned that I needed to account for everything. So, for example, I help my mother out sometimes. I needed to count that in terms of people I support.

Like so many Americans, Alexis must figure out privately how to manage the debt accrued from her PhD. She reported that her debt was no more manageable under the federal government's new Income Based Repayment program now that she had accounted for the costs of having financial responsibilities for her mother as well as her children. Yet she reported that she continues to struggle and noted that she has to forgo much needed dental and orthodontic care for her children and food for her family in order to stay afloat. Each time we spoke and her financial reality surfaced in the interviews, she was brought to tears. She always apologized and rhetorically asked, "Why do I always cry when I talk about this stuff?" For academic women like Alexis and the other women I interviewed, the imposed facade of performing the "strong Black woman" collapsed under the heavy weight of extreme debt and subsequent economic crisis, despite their ambition and PhD attainment.

In response to the United States' mounting $1.5 trillion educational loan crisis, many organizations have begun launching campaigns about the pitfalls of student debt. The American Institutes for Research rightfully cautions in the "Implications" section of its brief that we must take into account other contributing factors, including the distance students travel to attend graduate school, spending patterns during graduate school, the family commitments of doctoral students during graduate school (e.g., marital status and children), salary expectations after leaving graduate school, and even "students' inflated estimates of their future salaries" (2013, 9). I would reframe this latter point by suggesting that what might be inflated are students' assumptions that their educational institutions and elected officials have their best interests in mind and are not aiming to profit from the mismatch between their achievement orientations and their economic realities.

Public awareness campaigns exposing the high debt rates of Black college students and graduates have increased, and some offer solutions that focus on increasing students' financial education and literacy.[13] Yet there has been insufficient systemic response to address the rising cost of education and little mobilization from the generally "college bound" and complicit American public. Too few are questioning why financial institutions have been granted unregulated access to vulnerable populations in order to market high interest rate student loans and other student-targeted financial schemes, nor has the US government fully responded to why a college education in this country is no longer affordable to the majority of its populace. Proposed solutions that center on financial literacy are forms of gatekeeping and victim blaming in that they suggest people should not seek advanced education unless they can individually afford it. Thus universities and the state have successfully marketed an illusion of equity and access to underrepresented groups who are experiencing inequality while establishing partnerships with banks and financial institutions. These relationships are left unchecked and target a vulnerable yet highly motivated group of consumers that I term the "credential-seeking class." Even well-intended, policy-driven reports—such as those produced by Kaiser Permanente and the Center for Community Economic Development's *Lifting as We Climb: Women of Color, Wealth, and America's Future* (Chang 2010), which focus on educational debt as a factor in women of color's wealth disparity—fail to offer educational policy reform recommendations on curbing student loan debt, even though Black women are a growing contingent of the credential-seeking class saddled with such debt.

As these narratives and data reveal, economic barriers are substantial for many Black women graduate students. While many gain social capital from their degrees and claim space within higher education, this acknowledgment does not protect them from loan defaults and harassment from bill collectors. In addition, their persistence can often coincide with further indebtedness and the intergenerational transfer of inequity. For example, Alexis, a mother of two, recently graduated with her PhD and has a significant level of educational debt. She complicates the liberal rhetoric celebrating "having" a doctorate as a Black woman by discussing how the high financial investment in her education has produced a negative and unintentional intergenerational economic impact for her children. She spoke through tears:

> I've always told them, "Both of you are bright enough to have the grades to work your way through school." I've always expected that. But now, with him being thirteen and a half, the reality ... I'm sorry, I'm going to cry ... [pauses], the reality is starting to set in. I'm not going to be able to help him. I'm not going to be able to help him get to school, and that hurts [pauses] ... that really hurts. That really, really hurts.

When I asked her a clarifying question to better understand why she felt this way, Alexis explained that her imposed choices that produced high amounts of debt and low income were going to eventually lower her children's educational opportunities and wealth attainment. She concluded in a defeated voice, "Yes, and the thing is, in the end, it's going to matter. It's not mattering now because I'm able to cover it, . . . but it will matter later." Alexis's weighty clarity signals her understanding that her forced choices, like so many others, have intergenerational consequences.

Economic Repression of Knowledge Production

Once granted access to graduate programs, people of color, particularly women, continue to face a number of less visible barriers not readily calculated in the contemporary economics of pursuing a PhD. For instance, graduate students have been identified as an exploited "reserve army of workers" in higher education (Bousquet 2008), but even within this class, underrepresented women of color are the least likely to receive funding and opportunities from their institutions, according to a 2013 report by Kristina Zeiser, Rita Kirshstein, and Courtney Tanenbaum at the American Institutes for Research. In other words, they are less likely to be granted graduate assistantships and fellowships from their institutions. The dearth of funding opportunities available to underrepresented students also sheds light on the graduate student–led insurgency against graduate worker exploitation that has emerged within higher education in the past 20 years. This labor struggle has yet to fully mobilize around the issues faced by underrepresented groups, who are rarely awarded these potentially debt-defraying contingent labor appointments. Graduate worker activism has bettered academic working conditions across US higher education institutions for many; however, the data available on those who are most often granted these awards seem to suggest that these appointments have simply reinforced racial and gender privilege rather than transformed institutional labor practices that discriminate against underrepresented groups. Thus women and people of color are not benefiting fully from these hard-fought graduate worker labor victories, since these labor disputes historically do not engage the racialized and gendered dimensions of who assistantships and fellowships are awarded to in the first place, nor which instructors are vulnerable to disapproval and disrespect by students in the classroom and in the lab (Perlow, Bethea, & Wheeler 2014). They also do not engage racialized and gendered forms of labor imposed on women and people of color working in higher education (Nzinga-Johnson 2013). Thus, women of color doctoral students who do secure graduate teaching positions must then also deal with institutionalized forms of racism and sexism reflected by poor teaching evaluations, assumptions of presumed incompetence (Gutiérrez y Muhs et al. 2012), veiled forms of domesticated and subservient labor (Nzinga-Johnson 2013), and the often hostile school and work environment of the academy—issues discussed further in the next chapter.

These missed opportunities come into focus as underrepresented women of color doctoral students, particularly Black women, are most often forced to fund their doctorate through some combination of student loans, full- or part-time work either on or off campus, and personal funds. This was certainly the case for Charli, the woman who memorably likened the cost of getting her PhD to "mortgaging her brain":

> I have applied for fellowships, and I only got one summer stipend from my institution where I got my PhD. It's been very difficult for me to do the type of research I would like to do. A lot of times I have funded my research out of my pocket. It was very difficult for me to do the research that I wanted, to the capacity that I wanted, without those fellowships.

The women I interviewed also offered nuanced interpretations regarding the ways funding impacts their production of knowledge, especially those forms of knowledge that have been historically silenced within academe in marginalized interdisciplinary fields like ethnic studies and gender studies. Scholars conducting work on gender, race, class, or other forms of inequity using critical frameworks and discourses reported that their work was simultaneously scrutinized and underfunded.

Charli noted how having to rely on personal funds impacted the process and production of her research as an underresourced and self-funded doctoral student. She offered an example of how not having funds for books affected the production of her dissertation:

> So as far as research is concerned, I did my dissertation, for instance, I have less money for books because the libraries here didn't have what I needed. I did not have the money, because of the low pay, to get in my car and maybe travel over to the University of ———— and do the research work. So that was limiting. My institution has interlibrary loan, but there are times when you can't rely on interlibrary loan. Maybe I wanted to look in the archives. I've wanted to go to South Carolina and dig in some of those slave archives, but I just couldn't afford the plane ticket because I didn't have any funding and low pay. Meanwhile, you have gas. I've dropped some projects because I simply could not afford to travel and do the research.

This example is striking because it reveals the kinds of barriers so easily overlooked by traditional markers of enrollment, access, and completion. Unlike others denied access to pursuing a doctorate, Charli does have conditional "access," but her ability to forge a successful intellectual path within her field and her program is compromised by economic barriers that have intellectual and economic ramifications.

Family responsibilities and financial burdens are factors that delay or derail the completion of a doctorate if a student does not have support. It is no surprise then that African Americans, who often are responsible for caregiving at home and in the community, are reported to take longer to complete their degrees than any other group according to the Survey of Earned Doctorates (2012)—with a median 9.7 years for doctoral completion compared to 7.6 years for white students.[14] These delays in completion—which point to social and economic circumstances rather than intellectual ability—ultimately translate into higher educational costs and deeper overall debt for many Black doctoral students.

In addition to the known costs of a doctoral education for underrepresented students noted above, there are also "hidden in plain sight" costs that are informed by established race, class, and gender hierarchies within higher education. The nature of graduate education in a corporatized academic climate has intensified for all students in the past twenty years in that they are now expected, if not required, to teach, publish, and/or secure grants at higher rates in order to beat out the competition. Many current doctoral students are not only focusing on their degree completion but are leading or expected to lead professional lives similar to their professors. They teach, serve on journal editorial boards, publish, run labs, manage academic and other campus units, supervise staff, and represent their programs and institutions on various committees and via extracurricular forms of service at greater rates than ever before. Yet their labor largely brings prestige to their mentors and the university, not to overwhelming themselves as emerging scholars. If credit and advantages are given to students for performing these tasks—tasks made vastly easier when performed within a funded context—students with no institutional funding and fewer connections with faculty and professional networks within their fields of study risk further disadvantage. Thus, these often-concealed structurally and economically limiting realities render these additional expectations/requirements for becoming an academic overwhelming for many underrepresented and alienated women of color doctoral students.

Outsourcing Support

In order to keep pace, many contemporary doctoral students have turned to outsourcing their means of productivity and are paying additionally for their advanced education. This acceleration of productivity has bred new markets within the economy of higher education. For example, the insurgence of private businesses that offer professional assistance to underresourced and undersupported graduate students and faculty has grown exponentially in the past two decades. Statistical analysts, data analysts, copy editors, developmental editors, writing coaches, and professional/career coaches all represent such new avenues geared toward academic success and marketability. While we can rightfully argue that services such as copyediting have a long-standing professional history, a newer academic productivity industry has evolved partially out of the limits of universities that allocate few resources to properly mentor and socialize their newest and/or most vulnerable inhabitants—graduate students, junior faculty, and faculty of color.

It is widely understood that people of color and women are more likely to lack adequate mentoring or institutional support (Gutiérrez y Muhs et al. 2012; Turner & Myers 1999). Niyah, a doctoral student who was working on her dissertation proposal at the time of our first interview shared, "The one area I feel like I definitely need more support would be ... mentoring and having guidance through the process of completing the program and going into the job market." Niyah's anxieties are well warranted given that, in spite of increased enrollment, Black women are also more likely to have less personal income to pay for the aforementioned à la carte academic services. Yet in these intensified publish and produce or perish corporatized academic environments, they must use their personal resources to pay for developmental editors and other knowledge economy professionals to ensure that someone keeps them on track with their studies and, in some cases, simply even reads their writing and provides feedback prior to having to defend their thesis or dissertation. The increased pressure to hire an editor, a writing coach, or a webpage designer all come at an unaccounted for and undocumented cost, further exposing the multiple levels of inequity produced within the changing landscape of the privatized university. For instance, in my informal conversations with academic editors and coaches, several have shared with me that the majority of their clientele are faculty of color, women, graduate students, and graduate students and academics with children. These emergent "gray market" academic practices reinforce Black women's social and economic positions in society by producing an unnamed intellectual tariff for those enrolled in doctoral programs.

The rise of a privatized academic productivity industry also marks the transition away from the academic service and mentorship expectations of senior rank and tenured faculty who operate graduate programs. These changes are precipitated by professors' often forced unavailability to students, both undergraduate and graduate, owing to the intensified expectations in an increasingly hypercompetitive, entrepreneurial academic climate that they themselves are facing. Most professors, at research universities in particular, are charged to have active teaching, research, and community agendas. They are competing for grants to underwrite their professional pursuits, and for many, tenure and promotion are tied to the amount of funding they accumulate for their institution. Increasingly, professors are tasked with cross-marketing themselves on blogs, popular press websites, and personal web pages, although many of these emergent practices have been fraught with privacy concerns and political and legal upheaval. Granted, some of the stated practices represent efforts to reconceive the university without walls, but they also reflect the intensification and what I call the "extensification" of what it means to be an academic in an individualist and market-driven intellectual environment.

Persistent graduate students are learning to fall in line and dole out the cash, credit cards, and student loan disbursements needed to fund their degree completion. These platforms are not simply changes born out of the advent of new technology; rather, I argue they represent the rise of emergent markets driven by the limits of the modern university to accommodate its desperate and most vulnerable students and faculty. In the end, we are beginning to learn that they also signify costs that are not always calculated in the economics of doctoral education in the twenty-first century. In all of these cases, Black women, the vast majority of whom have less wealth as a result of long-standing economic inequality, have to make critical decisions about how far they are willing to indebt themselves and their families to pursue a life of the mind.

Pedagogies of Inequality

While legal barriers have been lifted, the rising costs of higher education have constructed subtle new forms of inaccessibility. For some women of color, these restrictions involve a painful process of having to give up on their dreams and "voluntarily" limit their ambitions. The experience of Brianna, a master's student, mother of a small child, and the recent author of a book of poetry, reveals one such structurally stunted trajectory. Brianna shared that she had been considering obtaining her doctorate; she relayed a conversation she had with one of her professors:

> We had a meeting last week and she just e-mailed me yesterday and she was telling me how proud she is and she knows that there's lot of room in the field and perhaps I could consider going for my PhD. And I considered it multiple times. If I had a position that was willing to pay for me to go get a doctoral degree, then absolutely I would. But if I have to fund it myself through loans, the chances that I would go to get it are highly unlikely. My student loans right now are around $71,000 for the undergrad and for the master's degree. A doctorate program may double that. I just don't know if the stress levels, as well as the economic issues [of] going for a more advanced degree would be worth it all.

The continued defunding of higher education and the subsequent rising costs limit the mobility of less resourced, intellectually curious students. It also creates a situation in which those students are trained just enough to be of service to the institutions where they study but not enough to demand more secure, well-paid positions, let alone to fully realize their ambitions.

Consider also the example of Tameka, an aspiring professor who was selected to participate in a faculty diversification program offered at her institution that funded faculty of color to prepare them to teach at colleges and universities. Tameka obtained her master's while in the program, which has enabled her to teach as an adjunct faculty member. Tameka enjoyed her experiences in the college classroom and wanted to continue her education by obtaining a doctorate; however, as the primary breadwinner and mother of two children, she believed the high cost of doctoral education has made her professional goal of becoming a tenure-track professor inaccessible. She confessed,

I've been there three years now. I'm only teaching one section. Full-time, I work for the [P-town] City School District. When I first started I was interested in going full-time because they had a position open up with political science that was full-time. However, they wanted me to have a PhD in order to apply. So when you start weighing out the costs to obtain a PhD, it was definitely something I reconsidered.

When I asked her whether she remained interested in pursuing her doctorate, Tameka responded,

To be honest, I've placed it on the back burner, just because I know that right now my focus is on raising my girls. I know they have needs that I have to meet right now, so I'm not able to go back to school financially. I think the biggest area is financial because I have been working two jobs.

When I asked her how she felt about having to make such a decision, she replied,

It's a disappointment. How do you tell someone you can't go after your passion because you don't have the financial means to do so? It's hindering me from pursuing something that I think I would be really great at. I enjoy it and it's a passion that I'll continue to do.

Notably, Tameka's academic labor continues to be welcomed on a course-by-course basis at her institution but with none of the job security or potential for advancement that a tenure-track, full-time position would offer. Tameka's structurally subjugated position reflects several compelling machinations of twenty-first-century higher education that are unpacked throughout this book. Of immediate relevance here is both the widening gap of who has access to higher education with funding, as well as the changing nature of being a college professor, a topic further explored in chapter 2. This trend is evidenced by the predominance of available adjunct faculty appointments over and above tenure-track faculty appointments, the rise in online teaching, and most recently, the steady uptick of colleges and universities promoting training courses and programs that offer certificates to people in higher education teaching. Prominent research universities such as Temple University as well as state universities such as Humboldt State University now offer a wide range of professional certificates that are producing an inherently limited version of what being a college educator entails, with little to no professional mobility for those who earn a certificate. This trend toward certificate completion has been highly controversial, and many view it as a signal of the profit-driven rise of credentialing over education within higher education. Nonetheless, it is a particularly concerning option for Black women, who as I will discuss in chapter 2, are disproportionately hired as contingent faculty even when they have earned a doctorate.

Faculty "training" programs, like the one Tameka participated in are ultimately institutionally self-interested, serving to maintain social hierarchies but sold as diversity initiatives. Their success lies in shoring up a reserve army of adjunct faculty that meet institutional fiscal needs. Programs that are targeted toward diversifying faculty, as was the stated intention of Tameka's institution, often produce forms of diversification that have no connection to deeper institutional transformation or social justice. Thus, Tameka's desire to advance beyond her adjunct post by acquiring a doctorate remains elusive when costs are at a highpoint and her institution's commitment to her education and career is at a minimum.

Most notable, Tameka's and Brianna's stories reflect the very real tension between the desire to pursue the work that one "loves" and the barriers that are present in the forms of financial and institutional inaccessibility. These contradictions expose both individualist and capitalist underpinnings of the popularized "doing what you love" rhetoric[15] or "diversification" and the actual forced "choices" that many Black women must undertake in their attempt to fully access the academy.

Conclusion

I began this chapter by arguing that our celebration of higher rates of completion for the doctorate is a market-driven neoliberal distraction from the material realities of highly educated Black women. A closer look reveals that Black women's higher enrollment into doctoral programs masks the doors that are most often closed to so many others and does reflect the financial gain for their respective universities and financial institutions. Furthermore, for those who do complete their doctorates, they often face a steep financial penalty and continue to struggle to transcend their social and economic position both inside and outside of the university. In this way, I argue, privatization limits the capacity to not only transform lives and fields of study, but also disproportionately obscures achievement and reproduces inequity for underrepresented women of color.

The testimonies shared within this chapter expose the material realities that many Black women doctoral students face beyond the seemingly rosy picture painted by statistics devoid of lived experiences. They also illuminate that which has been historically silenced by race and gender: the voices of emerging Black women scholars, who continue to forge paths toward access and equity despite twenty-first-century economic penalties. In spite of these modern-day institutionalized barriers to degree completion, Black women continue to demonstrate a strong and consistent commitment to education and its emancipatory potential. Yet the uneasy question of what happens next, once Black women scholars who desire an academic career persist, is addressed in the next chapters.

Chapter Two

Ain't I Precarious? Black Academic Women as Contingent

Perhaps my precarious employment would be more tolerable if my employer provided access to standard benefits such as health care, paid sick leave, and tuition reimbursement, but benefits are nonexistent.

—Wanda Evans-Brewer

In 2015 when I interviewed her, Dr. Wanda Evans-Brewer was a professor of English and literature, mentor, scholar, and academic labor activist. She had worked as a contingent faculty member at a private liberal arts university and a for-profit university. At the time, she was caring for her youngest child of four, a live-in aging parent who had cancer, and a spouse with a chronic illness. She earned her PhD from a for-profit institution, Capella University, and has six-figure student loan debt. She made less than $20,000 in 2015. In order to supplement the income she made as a contingent professor, she also was an Uber and Lyft driver, she rented out three bedrooms in her home, babysat, and received welfare assistance to make ends meet.

The income she made as a contingent laborer was inconsistent, and she did not receive employer-sponsored benefits that are typically extended to full-time professors, like health insurance, tuition remission, or parental leave. She shared that the for-profit university she worked for had not assigned her to any courses lately and her other university employer paid its contingent faculty half of their earnings eight weeks into the semester and the other half after the semester ended. There is usually a four-week gap between the fall and spring semesters and a twelve-week gap between the spring and fall semesters. Like many academic institutions that use a "flexible" workforce model, her employers at the time offered their contingent faculty courses on a semester-by-semester basis. Wanda reported that her employers had reduced the number of courses that they typically offer her to teach.

In response, she decided to apply for unemployment insurance through the state of Illinois, since she would have to go for a long stretch without pay with no insight as to whether she would be offered classes to teach for the following semester. When she received confirmation from her employer that she would be offered a course to teach for the next semester, she canceled her unemployment insurance. She reported that she was forced to make the decision to apply for unemployment only out of desperation in order to feed her family and keep her home, but her choice was considered fraud by the state of Illinois. Subsequently, the state of Illinois sued Wanda for $4,000 and ruled that she could not receive unemployment insurance in Illinois for two years.

Wanda's case is complex but is important to highlight, given that she experienced both precarious employment and legal ramifications simply from attempting to pursue a career as a professor. Yet the lawsuit by the state of Illinois implies she was dishonest and an exploiter of state resources and employment policies. The adjunct labor crisis generally has drawn public sympathy in the press, but Wanda's criminalization as a Black woman signals an old and familiar trope of the "welfare queen" who is always trying to "beat" the system. These ironic and painful parallels were not forgotten by Wanda, who expressed her resulting emotional and financial distress. She also noted that no one at her employing institution came to her defense when she asked for a letter to help explain her circumstance. The New Faculty Majority (2018) has launched a campaign to support adjuncts like Wanda who wish to collect the unemployment insurance benefits they are entitled to, but Wanda's case exemplifies how vulnerable adjunct workers are when academic institutions, legislators, and state unemployment agencies are not responsive to the plight of contingent workers as well as the compounded vulnerability of Black women in higher education workplace settings.

Many full-time academics, like many middle-class people, may try to distance themselves from such racialized, classed, and gendered labor struggles. But the contractual contingency that comes for growing masses of part-time faculty members in the morning has already been coming for vulnerable women and people of color faculty at night for some time now, regardless of their contract. Such was the case of Monique, which offers a glimpse of what has been at stake for structurally contingent tenure-track and tenured academics who hoped they are at least contractually safe from the latest vices of academe. When I interviewed Monique, she had recently relocated for the second time in less than twelve months.

In the previous year, Monique's qualifications helped her rise to the top of the short list of candidates vying for a highly coveted tenure-track faculty position in sociology. She impressed the campus search committee over the course of her two-day interview. She was then invited to join the university as a tenure-track assistant professor with a starting date in the fall of 2013. At the end of her first year of working as a tenure-track professor, she was called into her institution's vice president's office. The vice president, by command of the university president, informed her that she would not be invited to return to the university the following year. During Monique's first year toward becoming a tenured professor, she had been laid off.

The president of the university justified his decision by disclosing that the university was in fiscal danger because of declining enrollment and decreasing endowments. Although her department generated the second-highest revenue for the institution, the vice president stated that Monique was being let go because she was the last faculty member hired. Monique soon discovered that the president had made an executive decision to balance the institution's budget by "trimming the fat" of faculty, without the knowledge or approval of the board of trustees. However, once the board of trustees was made aware of the president's actions, they did not contest or reverse his decision. And so, it was that Monique and several other tenure-stream faculty members found themselves suddenly unemployed.

The university president's reported belt-tightening was not the only strategy he used to balance the institution's budget. At her point of hire, Monique became one of three African American faculty members and one of two African American women tenure-track faculty members to work at the university. She reported that she had been hired as part of the university's latest diversity initiative. She reported that the other tenure-track African American woman was a successful senior colleague who taught for years at the graduate level in another department at Monique's institution. When it came time to balance the budget within that department, Monique's senior colleague was first asked to teach only undergraduate courses, but she reported that her colleague attempted to reassert her seniority and refused this unprecedented "demotion." In response, the university administration then gave her the "choice" to retire with emeritus status. She accepted their imposed choice and retired early in the spring of 2014. Her former department subsequently contacted her over the summer because they were short on teaching faculty. She was invited to teach courses as a "just in time" adjunct, with substantially lower pay than she had received as a tenured faculty member in the same department the prior academic year. Monique shared that her former senior colleague declined the university's last-minute offer. Thus, Monique's former institution began its 2014–15 academic year with no African American women professors and with a sole, male African American professor on its faculty. These factors drove Monique to question the institution's stated commitment to diversity, particularly with regard to Black women.

When the fall 2014 semester began, Monique was relieved and excited to begin a new full-time but contingent faculty position at another university. Her colleagues have been welcoming, but this does not erase her awareness that her contract is renewable year to year and not tenure-track. She noted that she was earning less income but with a higher cost of living. Monique also faces looming graduate student loan debt repayment, which has forced her to pick up an additional teaching position with an online university. She remains traumatized by the circumstances surrounding the sudden loss of her former tenure-track position but expressed an all too familiar "hope" that her current contingent position could possibly become a tenure-track post in the future. Most notably, Monique reported simply being happy to have her own office as a new academic year begins.

Contingency in All Its Multiplicity

"Contingent" is an umbrella term that generally encompasses a multitude of contracted non-tenure-track faculty positions including adjunct, clinical, research, graduate student workers, and other flexible academic workers. The rise in higher education's restructured corporate managerial practices and late capitalist business partnerships with the private financial sector, the military, and private prison industries have had deleterious effects on both faculty and student lives with the expansion of a contingent academic labor force (Olssen & Peters 2005). With regard to student outcomes, one statewide study comparatively explored their educational pathways based on whether they were taught by contingent faculty or tenure-track faculty. Xiaotao Ran and Di Xu (2018) found that while having one's introduction to a field of study taught by a non-tenure instructor is on average associated with a higher course grade, students in this circumstance were less likely to attempt another course in the same field, and among students who did so, non-tenure faculty in introductory courses also had negative impacts on students' next-course performance within the same field of study. The positive impacts on current course performance and negative impacts on subsequent outcomes are especially strong among short-term non-tenured faculty. One potential explanation for this result is that adjunct instructors, especially those employed on a temporary basis, due to job insecurity, may reduce the difficulty of course content, lower course expectations, or relax grading criteria in order to earn good student evaluations. These findings are important because they draw connections between grade inflation, student interest in choosing majors, and the vulnerability of adjunct faculty members.

With regard to faculty, one of the most destabilizing practices of the corporatized university has been the wholesale adoption of a profit-driven business model, which configures faculty appointments as inexpensive and disposable positions crafted to meet budgetary and market demands. There has been a 376 percent growth of non-tenure-track faculty positions over the past 20 years and a severe drop in full-time tenure-track positions during this same period (Schuster and Finkelstein 2006). The US Department of Education's 2009 Fall Staff Survey reports that 75.5 percent or 1.3 million of the almost 1.8 million faculty members in the United States are now working as contingent contract professors.

This flexible army of faculty members includes all demographics, but women and people of color have faced compounded forms of vulnerability within the neoliberal university (Marginson 2006; Osei-Kofi 2012; Schell 1998). According to the American Federation of Teachers (AFT 2010), "underrepresented racial and ethnic groups are even more likely to be relegated to contingent positions; only 10.4 percent of all faculty positions are held by underrepresented racial and ethnic groups, and of these, 7.6 percent—or 73 percent of the total minority faculty population—are contingent positions." While compensation is deplorable for most contingent faculty members, the Coalition on the Academic Workforce's (2012) data indicate only a slight variation in median pay by gender: women reported a median per-course salary of $2,700, and men reported earning slightly more, at a median per-course salary of $2,780. Race or ethnic breakdowns suggest that part-time faculty respondents who identified as Black (not of Hispanic origin) earn considerably less than other racial and ethnic groups, with a median per-course salary of $2,083. The median for Latino respondents was $2,500 and $2,925 for Asian or Pacific Islander respondents.

In addition, it is important to note that the vast majority of tenure-track Black professors are employed at Historically Black Colleges and Universities (HBCUs). Those who teach at predominantly white institutions are overrepresented as contingent faculty and are less likely to have tenure. Black non-Hispanic contingent laborers are also somewhat overrepresented at two-year colleges and underrepresented at doctoral universities compared to other groups. Together these findings point to both the casualized employment landscape that all academics are currently navigating and the historic forms of inequality reproduced by institutional racism that is all too familiar to Black academics.

Wanda's and Monique's stories reflect more than just the seismic shift in the academic workforce over the past twenty years. In fact, their separate but interconnected circumstances offer us compelling examples that complicate dominant notions of contingency and disposability in higher education. Their compounded disposability, and in Wanda's case criminalization, reflect the contradictions of colleges and universities that claim to be championing diversity, equity, and inclusion, while simultaneously pursuing institutional labor practices that disproportionately impact marginalized populations—practices, furthermore, that have a much longer history and politics than many current analyses would suggest.

A critical literature has emerged that traces the casualization of the academic workforce as it has ostensibly devolved from a relatively stable profession into a largely precarious and bifurcated labor force with wide disparities between tenure-track and non-tenure-track faculty (Bousquet 2008; Donoghue 2008; Massé and Hogan 2010; Newfield 2011; Schell 1998). Yet a growing number of feminist, postcolonial, and critical race scholars have noted that these "shifts" have always been in place for underrepresented minority faculty like Wanda and Monique, and for fields of study that rose out of modern social movements in the United States, despite claims regarding the now "diversified" university that would suggest otherwise (Ahmed 2012; Chatterjee and Maira 2014; Ferguson 2012; Mohanty 2013). Historically, these subjugated academics have been considered and treated as disposable and even criminal regardless of their promise, their contributions, their appointment status, or even their seniority. How should we then think about forms of disposability and contingency that continue to be reproduced (but narrated as "new") by institutionalized forms of racism and sexism within academia?

This question is critical as Black women academics face positions of sustained precarity that are demarcated by their disproportionate overrepresentation as underpaid lecturers, adjuncts, skills course instructors, and assistant professors. The US Department of Education reported that in 2009, although there were 6,411 Black female assistant professors employed at colleges and universities in the United States, there were only 2,331 Black female faculty who were full professors. Conversely, there were 49,650 white female faculty members working as full professors during the same time period (2011, table 315.20). Despite higher education institutions' professed commitment to diversifying faculty in higher education, this disparity in numbers between assistant and full professors has been attributed to the disproportionate number of Black female professors who have been denied tenure by their institutions or not offered tenure-track appointments at all (Turner & Myers 2000).

In addition to the dearth of noncontingent appointments occupied by Black women, they are also more likely to lag in pay, resources, benefits, and the protections of collective bargaining units. As mentioned earlier the Coalition on the Academic Workforce (CAW) reported that non-tenure-track faculty respondents who identified themselves as Black (not of Hispanic origin) earned significantly less than other racial and ethnic groups at a median per-course pay of $2,083, and this was the case even when the type of institution was included in the analysis (CAW 2012, 12, table 31). Black faculty who participated in the study were also more likely to be employed in the southeastern United States, where pay rates are

generally lower and there is substantially less union representation for academic laborers (CAW 2012).

The persistence of these multifaceted labor-related injustices indicates that Black women's permanence within the ranks
of faculty remains precarious. What is historically relevant in
these now well-known findings is that these numbers have remained unchanged for underrepresented faculty in higher education before, during, and after corporate restructuring in
higher education. For example, a 2012 National Center for Education Statistics report revealed an almost 43 percent increase
in the award of PhDs to Blacks—from just under 7,000 in
1999–2000 to slightly over 10,000 in 2009–10. Yet, the average
increase in Black faculty appointments at predominantly white
institutions during the same time frame was only 1.3 percent
and is currently only 4 percent overall and 2 percent for Black
women specifically. Thus, it remains evident that women of
color academics, particularly Black women academics, live and
work precariously across broader economic crises, labor market fluctuations, and political shifts in leadership in the United
States.

These data call for more nuanced analyses and perspectives
about contingency and the ways in which the neoliberal university operates not as an equalizer, but as a *reproducer* of inequity
for women of color, despite their high levels of education, intellectual contributions, and professional potential. Furthermore,
investigating the institutionalized production and reproduction of inequity is urgent and relevant not only for the light it
will shed on the situated experiences of Black women contingent faculty but also for what it can tell us about how the
university operates in the neoliberal era and across time.

This chapter begins by offering a historical analysis of academic labor conditions that charts and contextualizes the "recent" shifts in university labor structures and the mounting

resistance against such changes. It then re-centers the multi-plicity of Black women's experiences as both contractually and structurally contingent. It is important to distinguish be-tween these two interconnected forms of contingency. I argue that faculty of color, particularly women of color, are *contrac-tually contingent* under the university's latest restructured formation—an employment status shared with their white academic counterparts, who are similarly subject to job inse-curity, lower wages, poor work conditions, few or no benefits, and little or no access to work-life entitlements—but within which women of color are disproportionately represented. But, in addition, I argue that women of color academics are also *structurally contingent* (and have been since their entry into academe), because regardless of their contracted ap-pointment status, they remain particularly disposable given enduring inequities (De Welde & Stepnick 2014) that are maintained and reproduced through institutionalized forms of racism and sexism within the university's academic work-force. I then turn my attention to the ways in which Black women's vulnerability is both ignored and compounded within the modern academic labor movement at this histori-cal moment. I note, for example, how the imagery and rhe-torical practices used by some within the current movement draw upon racialized, gendered, and class-based tropes to evoke public sympathy and incite mobilization. I then discuss the important, but all too frequently overlooked work of those scholars who *have* highlighted and critiqued what I name as "structural contingency," both historically and in the present context, and whose work provides the foundation for my own analysis. In the second half of the chapter, I counter the rhetorical silences and appropriations of mainstream labor discourse with situated narratives from racialized aca-demic women who are working as contingent faculty. Their circumstances offer us a nuanced window onto the many ways in which the university produces and reproduces inequity through its creation and maintenance of economic disparities, restricted professional options, and hostile intellectual spaces for underrepresented women of color.

The Invisible Labor of Gender and Race

As the labels of "part-time," "contingent," and "add-on" faculty suggest, non-tenure-track faculty do not have the full pay, rights, or benefits of tenure-track faculty, but these terms do not fully capture the amount of work contingent academics are expected to take on nor the work that they may be professionally or politically committed to. Historically, Black women have been especially committed to education as a form of racial uplift and social transformation, whether it entailed learning to read during chattel slavery or becoming educators dedicated to teaching across the educational life course from kindergarten to college. Despite and perhaps even owing to the changing landscape of the university, Black women academics are mobilizing in protest of the waning resources available to them and the students and causes they are committed to serving. However, these forms of sustained commitment ultimately also serve the capital gains of the university often at the faculty members' expense. Andrew Ross (2017) draws a similar parallel in his discussion of artist workers by noting that their sustained commitment to the work operates as a "cultural discount"—or an acceptance of nonmonetary reward or gratification for simply producing their art—in the absence of adequate compensation. Academic institutions are aware that many faculty members, particularly women of color, are committed to being educators and mentors within and outside of the classroom, and that they are resourceful. Thus, the often-stabilizing, retention-focused labor that is performed by those who are most committed to social transformation is frequently expected yet hidden and can be viewed as their "intellectual discount." Niyah described the student-centered work she participates in and how it matters but also how it is rendered invisible (and unpaid):

I had a student because she had been with me for three semesters, asked me to write her recommendation letter for nursing school. And I had to call her and say, "This letter is not going to work. I need to throw your essay in the garbage and start over. This is what your essay needs to say so that you can get into nursing school. I will write you a letter, but you need to rewrite this essay and send me your new application before you submit it to this school." I just told her. And my office mate was floored, but I told her because it was a young Black woman and because she had women's studies with me so I already knew what she was dealing with. Then she had some sociology classes with me, so knew her well. And I was honest with her. "They're not going to let you in nursing school with this application essay. If you want to get into nursing school, you need to say this and this." I don't get any compensation for that!

She then offered a detailed example of the length she goes to in order to retain her students:

I remember one semester I had a student issue that was like out of a movie. There were police cars everywhere. Now I know I haven't done anything wrong, but I had this feeling in the pit of my stomach, and I said, "I hope these police aren't here for me." I get to my classroom and guess who's at the door? Four police officers. So they said, "Miss ———, we need to talk to you." And I said, "Okay." "You have a student, Mary Jane, in your class and Mary Jane's boyfriend beat her up last night and set her on fire on purpose and he's threatening to follow her to school today and do something. So we'll just stand guard out here to make sure Mary Jane's boyfriend doesn't come." So Mary Jane's boyfriend of course has thrown her backpack away, thrown all her school stuff out in the street. So, I'm scrambling trying to find a new book for her so that she can finish the semester. Trying to get her new copies of all the documents, even though everything is online. Because I want to make it easy for her because he's destroyed her laptop. Checking in with her. "Okay, are you going to be in class this week? Do you need anything?" All of that kind of stuff. I don't get any compensation for that advising work. I don't get any compensation for those recommendation letters. I don't get any compensation for any of the mentoring, any of the things that would normally come with being full time. I don't get anything for any of that work.

Student crisis management cannot be predicted nor calculated as part of faculty responsibilities, even for tenure-track faculty; but Niyah's frustration about the extent of her undocumented and taken-for-granted labor in behalf of the institution and her students is notable.

Some might argue that she was not required to make additional copies or check on her student who was victimized by her boyfriend. Indeed, in 2013, a post by the pseudonymous contributor "Marni," titled "Adjuncts Should Do as Little Work as Possible," on the *Chronicle of Higher Education*'s *Adjunct Project* blog was ranked one of the top ten posts.[1] The author clearly wrote the piece in frustration at the state of affairs facing contingent faculty. Many of her readers agreed that doing less would be a radical form of resistance while others suggested, like Marni, that doing less would be in line with universities' increasingly profit-driven goals and the desire to pad their rankings. Others wondered if "doing less" was an ethical response and dismissed Marni's advice as shortsighted. Others pointed out that many adjuncts simply feel too vulnerable to take such a stance of "doing less," as they are well aware that any such efforts to regulate their own time could all too easily be interpreted negatively by their institutions and by students. During our interview, Niyah recalled the comments of one of her colleagues regarding the current knowledge economy of higher education: "My colleague once said, 'You don't know we're not here to teach? We're here to graduate students.' And I said, 'Oh, are we?' And she said, 'Yes, that's what I was told.' And I said 'Okay.' So that really hit the nail on the head for me." Yet, even with a keen understanding of the shifting purpose and intention of higher education, Niyah continues to engage at a level that goes beyond simply "graduating students." Niyah and the vast majority of the women I interviewed described a firm commitment to teaching and scholarship beyond that (misleadingly) associated with contingent faculty members.

In particular, women of color academics talked about feeling compelled to support those students who are underrepresented and often underresourced within the context of the university and society. This view was evident with Niyah, who stated her commitment to the predominantly first-generation, urban, and African American college student population. It was also evident with Marquita, who shared a class-based allegiance with her students. And it was also true for Cherida, who saw her students' academic success as critical to their survival in the United States. These women expressed both resentment of, and devotion to, the additional labor encompassed in this form of commitment to their students. In this way, the work narratives I heard offered nuance often missing from the mainstream discourse around contingent academic labor. In spite of the precarious nature of their faculty appointments, these respondents spoke of the work they performed with a sense of pride and dedication. Despite the lack of recognition they received for the various forms of invisible academic labor they performed, they continue to write letters of recommendation, advise students in everything from course planning to college applications, and help deal with issues such as domestic violence. Many of this group of Black women articulated broader interpretations of what it means to work in higher education. While they clamor to acquire a position from within, they also acknowledge an awareness of their position in society and by extension, the university's labor system. Drena offered a critical survivalist perspective concerning her choices to become an academic:

> That's something that women and Black women, we have always had to do. So, I think it's the norm. Not that that makes it any easier, but it's the norm, and I'm okay with that. I've recognized my position in society, and that I will always have to make those kind of sacrifices. I don't operate within the same privilege as some other women, because I acknowledge that it's part of my reality. That's how we operate and negotiate the choices we make as Black women. I'm okay with it because it's the reality.

The above narratives exemplify both the deep investment that many contingent faculty have for their students, as well as the legitimate sense of ambivalence and sometimes even resentment they feel as a result of being made invisible and exploited as workers. These narratives also highlight the slippery slope that is produced when stratified academic labor blurs the lines between social transformation and racialized and gendered exploitation. The "intellectual discount" they grant to higher education is notable, but their commitment to educational and social justice that rest outside of marketized frames offers a compelling counternarrative.

Excluded from the Ranks

Like many contingent laborers, the women I interviewed reported their strong desire to build and maintain connections within their respective fields and with other academics. Some expressed the realization that these possibilities are becoming more and more unrealistic given the crises in higher education that impose time constraints on everyone impacted by an intensified and corporatized work environment. Others acknowledged that these conditions create particular burdens on women of color who are often spread thin with enumerable duties. Yet, others reported attempts to foster professional relationships with their tenure-track counterparts. They are well aware of the disparities between their experiences and those of their relatively more privileged peers, yet they seek to find common ground and a sense of collegial solidarity. Niyah shared:

> *Actually, a lot of the time I feel distant because there's not a strong relationship that they build with their adjunct professors, at least for my department. I feel there's not enough full-time staff that reach out to the part-time staff. I know everyone has their own workload, I understand that. However, at the same time, because you don't see your colleagues on a regular basis, it would be nice if that relationship was developed.*

Such cross-professional connections can be difficult to find, however, and for some contingent faculty, their sense of segregation within their institutions can feel defeating. As Marquita noted: "Because add-ons really do feel like floaters. We just go teach the class and leave and we're never talking to anybody else you know.... I don't know, feeling like you're not a part of an intellectual community, 'cuz I don't really feel like that." These strained and segmented worker relationships deliberately keep academic laborers embattled and distracted from the actual focus of their connected labor struggles. Those who are contingent faculty have the most at stake and yet are the most impacted in terms of limited professional network building and increased vulnerability if and when they participate in labor mobilization activities.

The women I interviewed also talked about the deeper, long-term price of having limited autonomy to teach content that is beyond the foundational, skills-based, or diversity-related curriculum. Women and people of color are pigeon-holed into these devalued content areas that fall neatly into the production lines of the university's knowledge economy. Alexis elaborated:

> I feel like often there's two things: there's lack of traditional support, sometimes we're the last to be asked to collaborate. We're the last to be asked to present. I also feel like there is an attempt to pigeonhole in terms of, "Well, why aren't you doing research on this topic or area?" or "Okay, you're Black, so you can do the diversity course." Mind you, I'm doing the diversity course and I enjoy it because it's a course I enjoy, but don't think that's the only thing I can do. And don't try to pigeonhole me as like "Oh, she's a diversity person; great, we got a person in place, next step."

Women of color contingent faculty report that their own intellectual and professional aspirations are stunted under these controlled work conditions. Marquita shares: "Right after I graduated I started the add-on thing. It was composition-based, so, I'm like, I'm just teaching them how to write essays. It's not creative writing. I taught creative writing one semester, Intro to Creative Writing, and then I never taught it again. So I don't necessarily think I used that degree for anything I'm doing." Trice described a similar experience of feeling rail-roaded into teaching courses that were the least desirable in the department: "They wouldn't let me teach anything but speech classes. They arranged my schedule so that I was the first person in at 8:00 a.m. in the morning, and I was the last person out at night."

Alternatively, others celebrated having the opportunity to have more academic freedom as a contingent faculty member. Alexis noted:

The thing I've liked about being an adjunct here compared to being an adjunct at another institution is, I had a lot [of] freedom to make the class my own. As opposed to being handed the syllabus and being [told] you have to teach from this, and you can make small, grammatical changes, but this is what you have to teach from. So that's been really nice.

Alexis's experience was rare compared to most of those interviewed. Yet her sense of intellectual and pedagogical autonomy reflects the very freedoms that are under assault as academic labor continues to be casualized. These freedoms are not simply about independence; instead they are indicative of the many interventions faculty members, particularly underrepresented minority faculty, have developed in order to combat the hegemony of Western, patriarchal canons and methods that have historically been imposed on the classroom.

Despite often feeling buried by the teaching demands of their institutions, the women I interviewed continued to try to remain engaged in their profession through conferences and memberships. Cherida recalled:

We taught [a] 4-4 course load, and it was really difficult to write. I guess I could have if I really wanted to eke it out. But I was too busy trying to figure out how I was going to pay my mortgage and car note at the same time. But I was very active in terms of conference presentations. Always maintained my memberships, always presented at conferences every single year. Convened sessions, not only for the panels, but also organized some of the meetings.

Trice notes that despite her professional commitment, her economic circumstances often inhibited her ability to be fully engaged with her profession: "You know at one time I was one of the regional co-chairs for the NWSA [National Women's Studies Association]. I didn't even get to this meeting. That takes money. Where are you going to stay once you get there? So, I was active for a long time, and that wasn't that long ago. I'm not able to get to conferences because it takes money." She also noted the challenge of trying to remain intellectually engaged from her subjugated position as a contingent faculty member. She reflected:

> It was really hard to get [academic managers] to spend money on conferences and things like that because their bottom line was, it's not about student success or something about remediation. "We don't care about this women's stuff and African American studies stuff. That's your problem." So that was hard. They not only did not want to pay for it. They would say, "What do you mean you're not going to be at work for three days because you went to . . . We didn't really approve that." I held on as long as I could, still doing some conferencing and stuff like that. But it was really hard.

Experiences such as these illustrate vividly the structural constraints faced by contingent faculty, whose ability to develop as professionals, contribute to cutting-edge discussions within their fields, and develop career trajectories shaped by rhythms longer than a single semester at a time are constrained not by any explicit forms of exclusion, but rather by their enclosure within the lowest paid, least secure, and most disposable positions.

Limited Victories: The Academic Labor Crisis of Omission

Despite the rising tide of worsening academic labor conditions, faculty members remain the frontline workers of colleges and universities. They both shape and contest the culture of the widely revered American social institution of higher education. Feminist scholars have trained a critical eye on the restructuring and segmentation of the workforce in higher education. Feminist scholar Chandra Talpade Mohanty has argued that in

> the creation of a permanent underclass of professional workers in higher education . . . women workers of all colors in U.S. higher education are the hardest hit. . . . This is a slow but inexorable shift in roles, intellectual projects, and identity for faculty in higher education—and making the shift visible is an important way to read the operation of power and relations of rule in the academy. Here is one place where borders are being redrawn and discourses of retrenchment, funding, and efficiency mystify and cover-up the drawing of the lines in the sand. (2013, 179)

For more than two decades contingent faculty have been organizing and resisting the deteriorating work conditions and dwindling number of tenure-track positions at colleges and universities. They have organized by forming unions and by collectivizing as colleagues to make demands upon their individual institutions, as well as to transform higher education as a democratizing institution. Additionally, scholars and professional organizations, particularly the Modern Language Association (MLA)—one of the earliest organizations to release a statement on contingency (MLA 1994)—have been critical of the downward trend of casualizing faculty appointments and have documented the negative impact of these actions on faculty governance and tenure (Slaughter & Rhoades 2009), academic freedom (Schreker 2010), the status of women faculty (Carr 2001; Massé & Hogan 2010; Schell 1998), the working conditions of non-tenure-track faculty (MLA 1994), and student learning (E. Benjamin 2002).

The current state of contingent labor conditions is often cast as an unprecedented or recent "crisis." Yet, Heather Steffan's (2010) analysis of the history of academic labor reveals that academics in the early twentieth century were mostly untenured workers who were primarily fighting for better pay. Academics later fought to be recognized as a profession and to be respected on par with other professions such as doctors and lawyers. In these ways, the current mainstream academic labor platform shares these early-twentieth-century intentions regarding the maintenance of middle-class professional values and the preservation of an academic elite culture that is primarily concerned with professionalization, intellectual autonomy, and the stability of full-time employment.

Their elitist aspirations notwithstanding, it is important to note that early academics fought valiantly for the establishment of employer-sponsored entitlements, the standardization of the tenure and promotion processes, stronger faculty governance, fairer and safer academic labor practices, occupational safety, and academic freedom. These laudable workplace victories allowed predominantly white, male professors to maintain their patriarchal positions in society, as well as in their homes, as primary breadwinners of heteronormative, middle-class family systems. These victories also enabled them to erect a masculinist and individualist work culture that also entailed a distancing from blue-collar workers and a reassertion of white, male, middle-class power and privilege in the workplace. However, once women and people of color gained greater access to the university following the gains of the mid-twentieth-century civil and women's rights movements, these now established white, male colleagues and networks—now enjoying seniority through tenure and/or administrative posts—did not collectively mobilize with the same intensity to advocate for inclusive and just labor standards such as creating nondiscrimination policies and practices, developing maternity/family leave, creating practices that value and equitably distribute institutional service labor, or enacting comparable worth pay policies (De Welde and Stepnick 2014). Instead, history reveals that they were often at the helm of ensuring the academy maintained its exclusionary work culture that kept scholars of color and women, as well as the knowledge production interventions they often brought with them, at bay.

For instance, a report prepared by the Graduate Student Employees Organization (GSEO) at Yale University, titled *The Unchanging Face of the Ivy League* (2005), reveals the exclusionary, racist, and sexist labor tactics and strategies that elite universities in the United States have historically upheld. Despite protest but without penalty, these institutions continue to reproduce class privilege both at the faculty and student level. The report notes that faculty of color and women continue to be systematically hired as contingent within the stratified labor structure of Ivy Leagues, but it should be noted that these stratifications can also be seen across all levels of US higher education institutions. Additionally, in her 2010 essay about gender and service in higher education, Mary Burgan reflects on how the highly gendered, domesticated roles played by "pre-feminist" academic women of the 1960s served to maintain male-dominated academic departments: "The women of my pre-feminist generation were among the first to benefit from the 60s dawning awareness of the need to diversify the professoriate, but they also entered the academy with a sense that their security would be unsteady there" (2010, 24).

In other words, while women, especially white women, benefited from gender equity legislation and policy, they nonetheless entered the academy only to find their own set of workplace challenges as both contingent and gendered workers. Forty years later, as evidenced by Monique's termination from a tenure-track position, women and people of color remain overrepresented as alarmingly disposable contingent faculty. Additionally, racialized women remain extremely marginalized and are the least likely to benefit from either civil rights legislation or gender equality policies within the university as well as within society at large. Their labor is devalued and overrepresented in service to the institution, with little reciprocity in terms of institutional commitment to their permanence.

While modern academic labor struggles are critical in reclaiming the university, the genealogy of academic labor struggles should be understood within a continuum that includes both victories and setbacks for racialized, gendered, and other social outsiders. For instance, the civil rights and modern social movements from the mid-twentieth century onward were hugely influential in transforming the university as a social institution. Ethnic studies programs and departments were first established in the 1960s and 1970s as a result of multiethnic student and faculty activism at many universities (Karabel 2005; McMillan Cottom 2014a). These hard-fought intellectual spaces were often poorly resourced, understaffed, co-opted, and met with political and ideological resistance from university administrators (Ferguson 2012; Mohanty 2013). Such historically politicized and interdisciplinary fields of study remain chronically underfunded, understaffed, and under political and economic attack contemporarily by the institutions that were forced by prior generations of student and community activists to establish them. The often-precarious status of area studies programs and interdisciplinary fields also exposes their vulnerability of being institutionalized within a system founded on the very hierarchies and economies that many scholars within these fields seek to challenge (Mohanty 2013).

I foreground these continued academic labor struggles to reiterate that faculty of color, particularly women of color, regardless of appointment, were never intended to belong to the academy—or perhaps, to put it more accurately, the academy was never meant to be a space for the development and enrichment of such faculty. In the twenty-first century, they remain what I refer to as "structurally contingent"—a stratified labor position related to, but distinct from the "contractual contingency" that has increased for all academics as a result of the neoliberal defunding of higher education and the subsequent casualization of the academic workforce. Whereas contractual contingency can be discussed in terms of academics as a labor category within the university's hiring structure, the structural contingency that I identify is something historically and disproportionately a designation for those whose labor is already marginalized and underrepresented *within* the academic workforce—those, one might say, who are systematically disposable. I underscore this assertion by noting the historically low numbers of people of color as faculty (both tenure-track and non-tenure-track), the low rate of senior faculty of color posts, their high tenure and promotion denials, their overrepresentation in teaching posts, and the systematic undervaluation of their scholarly and creative productions by institutions of higher education. Finally, faculty of color, particularly women of color faculty, can be and have been exploited through their overrepresentation in gendered and racialized servant labor, and rendered institutionally vulnerable by their disproportionate placement in area studies and interdisciplinary programs that are being disbanded en masse as academic institutions restructure.

It has long been argued that the tenure and promotion process is one of the most effective strategies in maintaining a largely white and male ruling class in the academy, which has been deployed as a form of affirmative action backlash against racialized faculty members (Patitu and Hinton 2003). The same men who earlier fought for job security by establishing the tenure and promotion process in the first place continue to be largely responsible for deciding who can now join their ranks as tenured colleagues. This has been a key strategy since the institutionalization of affirmative action in higher education, a development not so coincidentally aligned with the increasing productivity expectations for tenure-track faculty (Hanks et al. 2008). In addition, countless scholars have noted that women and people of color academics remain vulnerable as a result of the sheer amount teaching and service demands that are placed upon them while in the tenure and promotion pipeline (Cox 2008; Harley 2008; Nzinga-Johnson 2013; Turner & Myers 2000). Finally, as Monique's experience and that of others like her reveals, even when people of color attain access to the tenure and promotion process, their structurally contingent stratification within higher education renders them disposable.

The American Federation of Teachers' (AFT) recent report on the diversification of faculty by race identifies a host of obstacles facing underrepresented minorities, including barriers to the educational pathways that lead to becoming a faculty member, bias in the hiring process, and institutionalized inequities in the retention of faculty members (2011, 7). Chapter 1 highlights many of the impediments faced by Black women graduate students by exposing how privatization of higher education has produced new barriers and penalties that have compounded their marginalized position. These obstructions are not traditionally framed as labor issues, yet they reflect the systemic and longitudinal nature of labor struggles that underrepresented women face before, during, and after their employment. Yet, despite these barriers, faculty of color continue to bring profit and prestige to their institutions under the cloak marketed as progress. These oft-overlooked barriers and precarious labor conditions that situate labor within the racialized and gendered landscape of the academy are crises—though hardly altogether new ones—for underrepresented minority academics. Corporate restructuring now intensifies the disposability of faculty of color, but it also persists in its historic forms. Reflecting on her work with Black academic women, Tressie McMillan Cottom reminds those who are mobilizing around the current adjunct crisis to look critically at their efforts and whose interests are being served—and ignored. She writes:

> Last year, I moderated a panel on black academic women's health in the academy. The administrators were overwhelmed by the intensity of response. Hundreds of essays poured in about the racism and sexism that stymied their academic careers. Many felt silenced by faculty groups that were supposed to protect them, ignored by comrades in the adjunct struggle who did not address how racism compounded its effects, and exhausted from straddling so many worlds. (2014a, 2)

Thus, for Black academic women and other marginalized faculty, contingency is informed by established racial, class, gender, and social hierarchies embedded in the social, economic, and political infrastructure of US higher education institutions.

Budgeting for Conditions of Failure

Today's flexible and disposable academic labor force faces a host of concealed exploitative working conditions. These conditions are coercive in nature and often force or compel non-tenure-track faculty to perform tenure-track faculty duties without the corresponding pay or promise of job security. In addition, racialized women are often positioned as institutional servants, and though they often act outside of and in resistance to the culture of capitalist and imperialist dominance that US universities uphold, they also serve as stabilizing forces within their respective institutions. For instance, students who know little of non-tenure-track faculty members' contract status often turn to those faculty members for support and services that are outside of their contracted (and compensated) duties. Niyah offered critical insight into the murky understandings students have about faculty posts, as well as the invisible but institutionalized forms of labor that result:

> *It's embarrassing because you do all this work and you get miniscule rewards, right? It's embarrassing. It's also outrageous in the sense that you have all of these requirements to do this kind of work, as if doing this kind of work is a privilege. That's the only way I can think of it. And in the midst of that, you are penalized. You are not going to be paid what you actually are earning by doing adjunct work. You're not getting good pay for the prepping of class. You're not getting paid for the recommendation letters you write. You're not gonna get paid for the after-school stuff. Every semester I have, "Miss ———, what are you teaching next semester?" I tell them when I am teaching something, but I've been at the university for two years.... I have some students that have been with me that entire two years, and they want recommendation letters. I tell them the facts. Are you sure you want a recommendation letter from me? I'm not a full-time faculty member. Right now, I'm teaching summer school, but over half my class is the football team. It's because they just got out of high school, they have to come to college to start conditioning to play college*

football. Part of ensuring that these athletes graduate is that they go to summer school every summer. Half of my class is the incoming freshman line. I pretty much have to check in with the athletics department every week. I don't get paid for keeping track of how the football team is doing compared to the rest of the class. I know that they're gonna e-mail me and say, "Hey, how are the guys doing? Are you having a problem? Need anything?" So that's an extra e-mail that I've gotta answer. And I really do have to go through the roll and see if the football players are coming to class. Right, it's extra labor.

It is perhaps unsurprising that such distinctions between faculty appointments are unfamiliar to students, but sometimes even tenure-track faculty members belittle, profit from, and/or ignore their colleagues' stratified labor positions. Niyah described one such interaction:

I remember someone in the Black PhD group on Facebook. They were going on this self-righteous rant about, "You are an adjunct. You are hired to teach. I am a full professor so I have to do A, B, C." So, I was like, "Well, I understand you're a full professor. You are paid for these things, this is part of your job description. But students do not understand that, and they don't know that. So yes, as an adjunct I still end up writing recommendation letters. I still end up sitting with students counseling them, advising them on what classes to take. Giving them extra materials if they're nervous about a class.

Far from fostering a collegial environment then, the university, on the one hand, obfuscates inequities among faculty from the view of students and the public but, on the other hand, benefits from the hierarchical, internally divided workforce that results.

In addition to the scarcity of economic resources and hectic pace that often frame their work lives, the women I interviewed also echoed the widespread grievances of many contingent laborers concerning unwelcoming and inadequate work environments in a very literal, spatial sense. One frequently reported complaint, alluded to earlier by Trice, was lack of appropriate spaces in which to prepare for class or meet privately with students. Marquita, for example, described the restrictions and confines of her work environment:

> *Even though there are a lot of add-ons teaching at the same time, we don't congregate in there. There's four computers in there, they're desktops, they're old PCs and no printer. We used to have a printer when I first started there, but they took them away because they said the add-ons were abusing the printer privileges, so now, now we have to go to the main English office which is kinda like adjacent, and they have one big printer copy and fax machine, and you, you're limited to ten copies. So, if you need any copies for your classes, you're supposed to outsource them to the printing shop, like 24 hours, or 72 hours in advance or something like that.... So, if you miss that window of print shop stuff, you're responsible for paying for that.*

When I asked Marquita how she felt working in this type of academic environment, she confessed:

> *It's not like a welcoming place where everyone wants to be. So, if you're in there working and you're not conferencing with students there, you hear everything that they're saying to their students, so there's no privacy or confidentiality in there. Which is interesting because I was reading this article in the* Chronicle *[of Higher Education] about, you know, the importance of professor offices, how they should be welcoming, and how kids should want to come to them. I usually conference with my kids in my classroom during our class. They come into the empty classroom with me, and then they go out so the other ones wait in the hallway, and we do it like that because I don't think they would like that, you know to be in there with everybody listening.*

Contingent faculty members' concerns for their students' privacy may spark creative solutions like Marquita's, but Trice's testimony in the previous section also reminds us that there can be life-altering consequences when contingent faculty try to ask for anything in return from their institutions.

The Unequal Impact of Neoliberalism in Higher Education

As illustrated through Monique's experience, even once they become tenure-track faculty, faculty of color, particularly underrepresented women of color, are at higher risk within the "flexible" economy of the corporatized university. Women of color academics and academic feminists have a long history of protest concerning the ingrained cultures of dominance within academia, but the political economy of the neoliberal university demands refined critiques. With the exception of a handful of academic labor activist scholars (Bousquet 2012) and a report published by the American Federation of Teachers (AFT 2011), very few academic labor platforms focus on the historic and structural inequities faced by women and people of color academics. The AFT's report on promoting diversity within the faculty notes that in 2005–6, approximately 5.4 percent of all tenure eligible and contingent faculty members were African American (2011, 6). When institutions are confronted with pressure to hire more underrepresented groups, they have done so through contingent rather than tenure-track positions. This evidence stands as a counterpoint to the smoke and mirrors generated by the tokenistic and still rare hiring of faculty of color senior scholars who bring widespread renown to universities. These minor, highly strategic maneuvers to "showcase" an institutional commitment to diversity distract from the needed structural interventions that must occur in order to genuinely transform higher education institutions.

The national trend toward hiring non-tenure-track faculty over tenure-track faculty constricts viable full-time employment options for all academics, but this is particularly the case for women and underrepresented minority faculty. More specifically, Gappa and Leslie's (1993) landmark study revealed that when Black faculty were hired, they were more likely to be hired as contingent rather than tenure-track, and according to recent figures from the US Department of Education (2011, table 31), this trend has held for the past few decades. However, as the casualization of academic labor becomes normalized, Black academics and other underrepresented faculty must now compete for the scraps of a contingent faculty appointment with more and more of their white counterparts. Thus, the enduring forms of racialized bias in hiring run the risk of being reproduced within the increasingly informal, subjective, and unregulated contractual hiring processes for non-tenure-track appointments. Additionally, while the contract terms of contingent positions are diverse, Baldwin and Chronister (2001) found that among underrepresented minorities, there was an 87 percent increase in the number being hired as full-time, non-tenure-track faculty members. This "smoke and mirrors" form of hiring underrepresented faculty fulfills universities' stated diversity criteria without destabilizing existing power structures and hierarchies. Such practices also expose underrepresented minority faculty to exploitation, as they often sound more promising than a traditional per course adjunct position and run the risk of coercing non-tenure-track full-time faculty to work harder in hopes of securing a tenure-track position.

There are a host of institutionalized reasons why such disparities in hiring faculty of color exist, but an often-overlooked component of the hiring process for non-tenure-track faculty points to its less systematic, less rigorous, and less formalized nature (E. Benjamin 2002; Waltman & Hollenshead 2007). For instance, many adjuncts are hired at the last minute and through already established professional networks. Numerous studies of people of color's experiences in higher education reveal that underrepresented minorities are often systematically excluded from these professional networks (Waltman & Hollenshead 2007). And despite being overrepresented as non-tenure-track faculty, the labor issues facing underrepresented minority faculty are typically framed as "goodness of fit" issues, which are, in turn, not recognized or prioritized by those leading other academic labor struggles.

Yet, given the proliferation of testimonies from contingent faculty as well as a now constant stream of blog posts, documentaries, YouTube videos, news articles, and books concerning contingent academic labor, one could easily conclude that these workplace conditions are both new and impacting faculty homogeneously (McMillan Cottom 2014a). These efforts indeed help in time-stamping and sounding the alarms regarding the massive shift toward the casualization of academic labor, but without historicizing the persistence of long-standing labor hierarchies within higher education, they risk disregarding the structural and compounded aspects of contingency experienced by marginalized faculty, particularly those of underrepresented women of color. They also risk thwarting the potential for building coalitions and momentum across academic labor struggles. It is critical to foreground critiques by noting that women and people of color have always entered into and prevailed within the academy under precarious and hostile labor conditions. For faculty like Monique and her senior colleague, the current labor crisis is simply a compounding effect of their historic disposability and struggles to claim their space within the university. Long before the current contract-based contingent labor crisis, Ann duCille (1994) reminded us that for Black women "the principal sites of exploitation are not simply the cabaret, the speakeasy, the music video, the glamour magazine; they are also the academy, the publishing industry, the intellectual community" (592).

For their part, feminist scholars like Eileen Schell (1998), Felicia Carr (2001), and Michelle Massé and Katie Hogan (2010) have all made valiant attempts to connect the gendered penalties incurred with the late capitalist move to normalize contingent faculty. Schell offers a definitive and prophetic study of the feminization of adjunct labor in US higher education in her 1998 book, *Gypsy Academics and Mother-Teachers*. Schell historicizes the social, economic, and political forces that shaped the rise of adjunct labor, particularly in the case of writing professors and the fields of English, literary studies, and communication and rhetoric. Her work, while limited to white women, is particularly important to women of color feminist critiques of the university because she creates space for women who teach as adjuncts to voice their own understandings of their work experiences, while acknowledging the structural challenges they face—but, importantly, she does not frame them as victims. There have been some documented victories, as noted by the proliferation of academic unions and contingent faculty organizations, since her 1998 publication, but by and large, the evident trend to increase contingent appointments over tenure-track positions suggests we have not benefited from Schell's forewarnings.

The 2014 documentary *Con Job: Stories of Adjunct and Contingent Labor* offers telling insights regarding who is most impacted, who takes up the most space, and who is omitted from the discussion about contingent labor struggles in higher education in the twenty-first century.[2] It is produced by two white, female faculty in English and writing instruction: Megan Fulwiter, a non-tenure-track faculty member, and Jennifer Marlow, a tenure-track faculty member. Yet even with women behind the camera and the fact that the majority of the non-tenure-track faculty sharing their stories on camera are women, the film mentions contingency as a gender issue only once, at minute 40 of the 45-minute documentary. Ironically, the masculine voice making the comment is also off camera, and the voice trails off after providing only a short sound bite but little substantive analysis regarding the gendered impact of the contingent labor crisis. Additionally, of the 11 academic labor experts who are called on to comment on the "academic labor crisis," 9 are white men. Conversely, 10 of the 17 narratives provided of people actually living/working in these exploitative conditions who are struggling to put food on the table are women. There is no discussion of the racialized impact of casualization and feminization of academic labor in the film. Additionally, there is little representation of faculty of color, despite their disproportionate likelihood to be working as contingent academics. Finally, a key focus of the filmmakers' critique seems to be the "preservation" of the professoriate as a somewhat romanticized category, which, whether intended as such or not, can be interpreted nonetheless as an elitist and individualist end goal, more concerned with preserving established hierarchies than challenging them altogether.

Only a few analyses have explicitly addressed the disproportionate impact of corporatized practices on women of color academics. These include Nana Osei-Kofi's (2012) critique of the "the overwhelming acceptance of neoliberal and neoconservative ideologies that advance corporate logics of efficiency, competition and profit maximization" (230) in the university. Osei-Kofi identifies junior faculty of color as the most vulnerable group in this context. There is also Roxana Walker-Canton's 2013 film *Living Thinkers: An Autobiography of Black Women in the Ivory Tower*, which chronicles the significant contributions of Black women in higher education in the twentieth century *despite* their precarious status. Through archival footage and the educational narratives of Black women scholars, the film simultaneously juxtaposes Black women's intellectual accomplishments against a race, class, and gender critique of the university's politics of disposability, which position Black women as undeserving outsiders. Finally, Marc Bousquet's (2012) analysis of academic labor market segmentation furthers Osei-Kofi's analysis of the racialized effects of neoliberalism by arguing that these assaults on higher education have both a racialized and gendered impact. He argues that through the normalization and feminization of contingent faculty, higher education has enacted extreme economic penalties for women, especially those who are members of underrepresented groups, are in underpaid fields, and/or are employed at second-tier institutions or community colleges. Women of color academics most readily occupy all of these spaces and are extremely vulnerable to work-based exploitation and termination within the context of casualization of the academic workforce.

If, as I argue, women faculty and faculty of color have long struggled with issues of insecurity, contingency, and disposability in academia, one may well ask what accounts for the sense of sudden "crisis" running through so much recent commentary and critique. I agree with Felicia Carr (2001), who has argued that the recent groundswell of mobilization within adjunct labor activism can be attributed to the negative effects of corporatization finally reaching men, particularly white, highly educated men. As corporate labor practices have intensified and accelerated within the university, white men are now feeling the brunt in ways they have not widely experienced since the professionalization of academic teaching in the early twentieth century. White men, who have been historically positioned to occupy and "fit" within the hegemony of the academy, must now also face conditions of economic and professional vulnerability, and reliance on public and private support. Yet, despite the fact that much of their outcry seems to be a function of their patriarchal, highly gendered, racialized, and elitist sense of entitlement, their voices continue to dominate much of the current discourse about the contingent labor crisis—when it began, who it affects, and what should be done to address it. Professionally displaced and predominantly white men, many of whom were initially part of the ruling elite of academics or at least assumed they would be, are now mobilizing more than ever before. Others are showing up at union meetings to reclaim "the good old days" when they had power over faculty governance and also who had access to faculty appointments. Others are angry and disillusioned that they, too, have to scrape by and fight for tenure-track positions that have been casualized—just as women and people of color have had to do for far too long, without the collective backing of their privileged white, male counterparts.

Particularly galling (and telling) in this context is the fact that, in the face of these erasures from academic labor platforms and dominant discourse, the specific histories of oppression and labor exploitation experienced by underrepresented minority groups have been popularized and appropriated within mainstream academic labor discourse. In addition to confronting compounded inequity within the academic labor movement, we must also consider the rhetorical strategies and tactics of appropriation deployed within contemporary mainstream rhetoric. In the comments section responding to adjunct Maria Maisto's article, "Adjuncts, Class, and Fear," on the *Working-Class Perspectives* blog in September 2013, for example, one commenter, Chad Roscoe, wrote: "They can always just tell you they're short on classes for a semester and you're out, and the unions know and do NOTHING about it. It's not fear of looking like we're working class. We know we're not even working class; we're *slave labor*."[3] Such appropriation of historical imagery and discourse is not unusual in the contingent labor movement, and concerted efforts have been made to redirect these distractions to the critical work of labor justice in higher education.[4] Yet, these distortions regarding the placement of adjunct labor within the political economy of the university continue.

In 2014, former adjunct professor, now independent publisher, Victoria Hay was called on to defend the title of her then forthcoming book, *Slave Labor: The New State of American Higher Education* on the blog *Daily Adjunct*. Despite pushback from academic labor activists and critical race scholars regarding the use of racialized hyperbole, Hay, a white woman, unapologetically argues that "adjuncts can be said to be 'enslaved' by two sets of circumstances: a) their own choices; and b) the institution's choices."[5] But David Leonard (2013) counters that in using such language, unreflective white contingent laborers can often be "blinded by their cause, by historic myopia and often by the privilege of whiteness." This is most apparent with the use of terms like "academic slavery," particularly when paired with a failure to engage with or include the voices and perspectives of those groups that have most suffered from the impact of slavery and its social, economic, and political aftermath in the United States. Shonda Goward also offers an extensive response to this misguided strategy within the adjunct labor movement in her *Inside Higher Education* interview with Joseph Fruscione in his "Adjuncts Interviewing Adjuncts" column. She states:

> [T]he rhetoric around the adjunct movement, that frames adjuncting as slavery, is purposefully incendiary, and again marginalizing. I have been told that there is "no other way for us to be heard" and that sentiment makes it very clear to me who the "us" is and is not. No adjunct position is the equivalent of not having civil rights until just 50 years ago: meaning, in my family, I am of the first generation *born* with civil rights.[6]

Similarly, Tressie McMillan Cottom (2014b) reflects on the exclusionary effect of such racialized language and imagery:

> There is no labor movement without black labor. And I think a black laborer would be hard-pressed to find solidarity in a movement that so thoroughly and casually erases the history that made them less likely to attain a graduate degree and less likely to procure a tenure track job should they do so when the visible movement philosophers and organizers double down on calling a labor problem a slave problem.

These apparent platforms of omission make it difficult for faculty of color, non-tenure-track or otherwise, to politically align themselves with yet another struggle that does not appear to include their social, political, or economic interests. If institutional transformation and social justice is truly the goal, then adjunct labor struggles should be in solidarity with the labor struggles of marginalized faculty of color by centering the voices, working lives, and material realities of those who are disproportionately affected by the coordinated attacks—both recent and historic—on academic labor.

Similarly, Marc Bousquet (2012) has argued that academic feminists have not been collectively concerned with the casualization and feminization contingent of academic labor since they and the fields they are often associated with, such as women's studies, have become partially institutionalized. While I do not wholeheartedly agree with Bousquet's assessment, given the sustained history of feminist critique of higher education, he, along with others, exposes the quandaries of women's studies faculty in particular—a field that is itself both precarious and sometimes complicit within academic hierarchies. Importantly, some academic feminists have been vocal about contingency and corporatization. For instance, Minnie Bruce Pratt, in her 2003 keynote address to the National Women's Studies Association annual conference, spoke candidly about her own employment history of precarious appointments:

> Because from the beginning of my graduate school education until today—that is, for the last 35 years—the majority of my teaching jobs have been one-year teaching appointments, adjuncting for low pay, no health benefits, and, for a while, a job like my piece work on the assembly line, where I was paid per student. In fact, in my entire working life as a teacher until three years ago, I had never held an academic contract for longer than one year at a time. I am now on my longest contract—for three years. (Pratt 2004, 25)

Pratt continued by offering a structural critique of higher education. She reminded the feminists in attendance:

> And now we are living in a most extreme period of capitalist exploitation. Now, for us as educators, staff organizers, teachers concerned with issues of women's studies, we can see more clearly the connections between work life "outside" the educational system and work "inside" it, under capitalism. We can see the oppressions present in both spheres being intensified by the

drive for profits. We can see the ways in which universities are truly functioning as corporations.... Universities are hiring fewer and fewer tenured professors, and, like corporations everywhere, are cutting their benefits obligations by hiring temporary part-time instructors and in many schools using teaching assistants for the majority of teaching work. (Pratt 2004, 27)

Pratt's keynote charged her fellow academic feminists to mobilize around issues of class and contingency over a decade ago through her testimony and her analysis of the shifts in higher education. Her criticisms remind us that feminists have been vocal about these issues for quite some time. But at the same time, Bousquet's critiques remind us that academic feminists have not collectively mobilized around contingency, nor have they been at the center of contemporary larger academic labor struggles, despite the gendered and racialized impact on the academic workforce.

In a timely and promising development, I am currently involved with a committed group of academic feminists hailing from Puerto Rico, the United Kingdom, and the United States who formed a Contingent Labor Interest Group in 2014 to address contractual contingency as a pressing feminist issue within the field of women's and gender studies. One of our founding group's first efforts, spearheaded by Gwendolyn Beetham, was to propose conference sessions on contingency and create an online fundraising effort to enable more contingent faculty members and presenters to attend the 2014 annual National Women's Studies Association (NWSA) conference in San Juan, Puerto Rico. Gwendolyn also sounded the alarm by penning a "love letter"[7] to the field of women and gender studies to draw political connections and to activate our colleagues ahead of the 2014 conference. Once the coalition of non-tenure-track and tenure-track faculty convened, we proposed contingency-related resolutions for the organization's consideration. NWSA's membership passed the first resolution submitted to the governing council by our group, which stated "that NWSA shall initiate a contingency labor travel fund to allow support of those who are teaching as adjuncts to continue to have a viable presence in this organization" (NWSA 2015). NWSA's leadership also resolved to stand in solidarity with the 2015 National Adjunct Labor Walk-Out Day, an action that was planned for February 25, 2015.

The organization later released a statement of solidarity on February 9, 2016, which linked this academic labor struggle to the long histories of structural contingency and the compounded precariousness that so many others navigate.

> As the largest feminist academic organization in North America, the National Women's Studies Association (NWSA) is dedicated to leading the transformative and critical field of Women's Studies. Our members recognize that systems of oppression are interlaced and take seriously the material conditions of knowledge production, labor commodification, workforce stratification, and structural inequities in educational practices. . . . The NWSA also underscores that the devaluation of academic labor, wage inequities, and disparities in hiring practices has been longstanding in the academy and connects to wider material and political contexts. Race, sexuality, social class, age, disability, gender, and citizenship are all factors that impact contingent employment.[8]

In addition, the 2016 NWSA annual conference was centered on the theme of precarity as a feminist issue.

Since the founding of the Contingent Labor Interest Group (CLIG), NWSA has worked to include options for its membership to sponsor feminists with less income and/or institutional support so that they can attend the annual conference.

CLIG, under the leadership of Julianne Guillard, has continued to organize panels and roundtables during NWSA's annual conferences. The 2019 conference, held in San Francisco
and themed "Protest, Justice, and Transnational Organizing,"
featured a host of sessions that signaled the continued legacy
of academic feminists who are mobilizing as labor activists. I
chaired CLIG's 2019 sponsored session at the conference on
"Feminist Labor Organizing: Collective Action for Academic
Workers." The conference also held two additional panels
that focused on contingent labor, including one session on
"Solidarity Activism: Building Bridges between Adjunct and
Regular Faculty" and another titled "Feminist Killjoys Organizing: Women of Color in Contingent Labor," which centered
on women of color as lead academic labor organizers. In addition, in 2015 several CLIG members published collaboratively,
as an act of solidarity across our contract designations, to take
up contingency as a political and intellectual issue within the
field of women's and gender studies. Our coauthored article,
"Women's Studies and Contingency: Between Exploitation
and Resistance,"[9] entered into conversation with a host of
other feminist critiques of the corporate university published
in a special issue of *Feminist Formations* coedited by Jennifer
Nash and Emily Owens titled "Institutional Feelings: Practicing Women's Studies in the Corporate University."[10] In sum,
academic feminist activists and scholars have been mobilizing
by linking contingency to a host of structural issues at stake
for women and other oppressed groups in higher education
and beyond.

During the same time frame, the New Faculty Majority, a
contingent labor advocacy organization, initiated a "Women
and Contingency" project in 2014, designed to examine
the gendered impact of normalizing adjuncts.[11] These recent
strides in recognizing the disproportionate inequities faced

by contingent women are laudable, but the raced, classed, and gendered blind spots of intellectual and feminist spaces that profess to center on dismantling these social hierarchies remain areas of opportunity in much of the emergent data on contingency.

My central critique of these omissions within current mainstream academic labor struggles and contemporary academic labor organizing is offered not to devalue the gains made by academic labor activists past and present, but to contextualize these gains and critically assess their unequal distribution, as feminists have long noted. I remain hopeful that the enduring academic labor struggles faced by women faculty and faculty of color are potentially reinvigorated now that the momentum regarding the adjunct labor crisis in American colleges and universities has reached all constituencies. For example, the US House Committee on Education and the Workforce published a 36-page report (2014) documenting the widespread deterioration of work conditions faced by contingent faculty. To the extent that the demands of exploited academic laborers are finally being heard, it is crucial to ask why those who are underrepresented remain marginalized, if not excluded, from the mainstream academic labor movement. Now more than ever, we need to listen to what these workers have to say about their compounded labor experiences of inequity in the modern university and to the feminists who are working at the intersection of race, gender, class, and academic labor.

On (Not) Landing the Job

Women of color enter academia with uncertainty concerning their future, despite their preparation for and commitment to their careers. They must navigate compounded forms of contingency because of the constrained nature of academic job opportunities, as well as the threat of being disregarded owing to their race, gender, and possibly even their scholarly focus if it is perceived by those in power as a challenge to hegemonic formations of knowledge production or established hierarchies. Combined, these intensified conditions shape every stage of their academic careers, including the job search process.

Charli is a recent PhD who was working as an adjunct at several institutions in an attempt to financially support herself and fund her research while she was completing her doctorate. She lives and works in the southern United States with her partner and child. Her research focuses on gender and race. During our interview, she attempted to make sense of her struggle to find a faculty appointment: "I can never be sure if it's because I'm Black and female, or if it's because I'm Black and female and I study masculinity. Sometimes I feel that it's related to the content." Charli's effort to understand her situation not only exposes the far-from-random ebbs and flows of a so-called job market that sees certain areas of study come in and out of fashion, but also questions the policing of bodies and bodies of knowledge that do not fit the neoliberal and murky categories of higher education.

Niyah also critiques the racialized and gendered forms of academic gatekeeping that inform bias in the academic hiring process. She is a doctoral student who has worked as an adjunct at an urban southern university for the past five years. In our interview, Niyah expressed frustration at not being able to acquire a more stable contingent faculty position. She recalled the expediency with which one of her less educated male peers gained a permanent position, and compared it to her own experience:

> He literally has his master's and taught two summer classes at this institution, and they're ready to roll out the red carpet and hire him.

I've been adjuncting at places for years and couldn't even get more classes as an adjunct, let alone a full-time offer. We are definitely penalized for being ambitious. That penalty comes out not just financially and with the departments we teach in, but also the departments that we choose to go to—or the departments that will have us. [Laughs.] There are multiple penalties.

Here, as in Charli's case, Niyah not only critiques gender and racial bias in the hiring process; she also ends by noting the intellectual enclosures that women of color face within higher education. Charli likewise shared her frustrations with trying to get hired full-time and noted the disregard she feels despite all the effort she has put into her career and her institution:

This place where I worked, from 2008 until 2013, let me tell you what happened with that. When I got my PhD, they had two job openings. I applied there for both of those positions. Even though I had been working there for five years, in those five years I had one or two bad student evaluation reports. Do you know that this community college did not even give me a job interview for those full-time positions? I noticed that in a lot of institutions, you are punished for getting a higher degree because they simply do not want to pay you.

Together, Charli and Niyah offer an integrated analysis contrasting their aspirations with the institutional devaluation of them as potential workers—something echoed in many contingent laborers' sentiments concerning the paucity of academic job opportunities. Yet, they also expose the complexity of their employment search in the restructured era of the university. Despite the rise in numbers of Black women with PhDs, as academic jobs are continually casualized, as the fields of study that women of color most readily occupy are perennially under assault, and while many historic racialized and gendered barriers remain, landing the job becomes a receding target for many Black women.

Just an "Add-On"

Once Black women have been hired as contingent faculty members, matters do not necessarily improve. When asked about the specific terms of their appointments, respondents discussed the precarious and patchwork nature of their jobs. When I interviewed Monique, she happily announced the promise of her newly acquired faculty appointment, but she also confessed that its duration was nebulous: "No, not a tenure-track faculty at this time. Full-time. The contract is one-year renewable. I think they do [such short contracts] until you get to three or five years. I should probably re-look at that, but it's that situation."

Other interviewees similarly recognized their diminished status in the academic hierarchy and reflected on the invisibility and disposability of their positions. Alexis is a new PhD who is working as a contingent faculty member and has begun to give up on the possibility of a tenure-track position. She was unsure if she even met the criteria for being interviewed as an academic. She hesitantly stated at the beginning of our conversation, "I'm only a part-time instructor. So . . . I don't know if that works for you." Marquita, on the other hand, struggled to find words to accurately describe the contract terms of her faculty appointment. As she put it, "I think I'm just an add-on faculty. I guess that's what they call them at this school so I'm *just* an add-on" (emphasis added). For both Alexis and Marquita, whether struggling to describe their own status or responding to the ways they are named by their own institutions, the message they must negotiate is clear: you are not valued, and you do not really belong here.

Many of the women I interviewed also reported the hectic nature of their lives and their need to work many jobs in order to make ends meet when they are hired as last-minute, "add-on" faculty—a burden experienced by many contingent faculty. Niyah tried to describe the pace of her day: "I would adjunct two days a week, and then I would go to the high schools three days a week for Kaplan and do ACT tests." Indeed, most contingent laborers point out that the income they receive is not a living wage in the states in which they live. Charli reported working as an adjunct from 2008 to 2013 and described the pay in her state as "some of the lowest you will find in the nation. It's $1,500/class per semester in this area." Thus, Black women who work as contingent academics and have acquired high educational debt (as detailed in chapter 1) find themselves facing many of the same precarious employment issues, economic stressors, and distressed labor conditions as Black women outside the academy.

Holding multiple jobs is reported repeatedly by faculty who work as contingent labor, but the specifically last-minute nature of many contingent hires is often overlooked, despite the fact that it produces for many workers a sense of precarity, instability, and often desperation. Charli's exasperation was clear as she explained this effect:

All of a sudden, someone left this other institution, so I was hired there part-time. But this institution was two hours away from my house, one way. I was hired to teach African American studies part-time. Then another local university called me. So I was driving two hours to this one institution on Tuesdays and Thursdays. On Monday, Wednesday, and Friday I was teaching part-time here in ———— at another institution to make ends meet. I was embarrassed because I still was not making enough money to pay student loans, pay the

car note and buy gas, and pay for my son's lunch and whatever school
expenses he had. I was not making enough money.

She also noted the chaotic and exploitive nature of just-in-time, part-time faculty hires: "The course load was supposed to be no more than three classes, but many times if someone got sick, or they had an explosion in student enrollment, I wound up teaching four classes." To counter those who might respond by arguing that at least she was teaching four courses, it is crucial to recognize that such last-minute contracts put adjuncts at a structural disadvantage, depriving them of valuable teaching preparation time, making them vulnerable to negative student evaluations, and generally increasing the likelihood that they will accept substandard conditions in order to simply have a job.

This on demand, just-in-time hiring compromises all contingent faculty members' ability to prepare adequately, but for women of color it exacerbates the already high risk they face of being perceived and evaluated as incompetent (Gutierrez y Muhs et al. 2012; Vargas 2002) or otherwise undesirable. For Black women, these work conditions within the university also justify racialized tools of backlash that academic managers can deploy against workers they deem unworthy or noncompliant. Trice has worked for almost a decade as an adjunct at several institutions in a large urban city in the Midwest. When employed, she spends a considerable amount of time driving from one institution to another. She described the punitive response she received from one academic supervisor after she attempted to ask for adequate work space for herself and her students:

Let me tell you what passed for my office. There was a space about
the size of your space that had a refrigerator in it and a microwave
and computer. So like your computer was on this desk, then along the

wall there were other computers that the students who took the class were allowed to use. So you could never come into your office and close it off so no one was there or leave anything that was private. I wanted to talk to her about that too. She would never meet with me. If I text you or call and you never get back, what choice have you left me? So I sent an e-mail and tried to explain to her that even in terms of students, sometimes to handle issues that they had, privacy was something I needed. That was in the fall. Spring comes she says, "You know what? If I had ever thought about making this position permanent, I'm not thinking about it now." So she just let the contract wear out.

The precariousness of a contingent appointment not only makes day-to-day work tenuous, but the nature of contingent contracts also compels workers to remain silent about their labor conditions or face backlash and possibly termination with no due process. For racialized women and people of color, such "new" corporate practices build upon an already long history of being silenced in the workplace and being deemed aggressive troublemakers on the job. With few alternative job options and worker protections, women of color academics remain especially vulnerable to discipline and termination under these intensified twenty-first-century conditions.

Mobilizing from the Margins: Black Women's Impact on the Academy

Before turning to the narratives of women of color academic laborers themselves, as I do in the following section, it is important first to recognize that women of color continue to subvert the political economies of contemporary higher education. One readily recognizable response to the historic practices of institutional exclusion has been women of color's persistence in pursuing advanced degrees and their navigation of the often-hostile landscape of the university (L. Benjamin 1997; James & Farmer 1993; Vargas 2002). Though their permanence has been transient and their attempts at institutional transformation have often been co-opted by powers that precede them, scholars of color, feminists, and postcolonial scholars critical of the university's practices of conquest and exploitation have offered formidable critiques of the aptly named "ivory tower" (Ferguson 2012; Gutierrez y Muhs et al. 2012; Mohanty 2013; Nzinga-Johnson 2013; Osei-Kofi 2012). The legacy of resistance of such scholars is evidenced by the transformative social justice work that many women of color perform on and off campus, as well as through their knowledge production and institutional building from within. These are political acts, acts of rebellion, regardless of attempts of co-optation that can and should inform our understanding of academic labor history. Collectively, they serve as critical accompaniments, if not predecessors, of modern academic labor uprisings, yet these histories of resistance and rebellion are often individualized, reduced, appropriated, and overlooked, and do not garner the same level of support from their colleagues.

The nature of precarious labor leaves those who perform it vulnerable to attack and work-based backlash. Not surprisingly, then, instances of individual faculty speaking back and naming the exploitive work conditions of contingent labor are understandably sparse. This is especially the case with faculty who are also racialized, gendered, or otherwise marginalized. Nonetheless, some Black women have offered nuanced insights on their compounded, stratified location as contractually and structurally contingent laborers. In "Teaching for Change: Notes from a Broke Queer Hustling Mama," Vanessa Marr poignantly analyzes how the corporate university's practices regulate her material reality but do not define her connection to her students as a Black woman academic. Marr explains:

I am not "required" to work beyond my teaching duties and office hours, I use these opportunities to nurture and build community to my advantage. I do not engage in these acts of compassion as a means of portraying myself as the self-sacrificing mammy hell-bent on burning out; rather, I am establishing what bell hooks characterizes as "homeplace." Not only does the classroom serve as a source of empowerment for my students and me to act on our own behalf, but it also provides a safe space to discuss social inequities in education and to engage on a personal level. When I explain to students what it means to be an adjunct instructor, many are shocked to hear that I do not have health insurance or that my income qualifies me for welfare benefits. They are curious to know how that can happen and why a college education doesn't automatically lead to material success. Some want to know how they can help, to which I respond: "Just spread the word that we exist and that we are struggling." When you hear that cuts to higher education are justifiable because supposedly all professors make too much money, remember us. Remember me. Then act accordingly. (2013, 69)

In addition to growing "homeplace" within the context of the classroom, Marr's work-life narrative continues by documenting the ways in which she builds community connections through what she defines as "queer hustling mama" pedagogy, which allows her to "transform current positions of powerlessness among oppressed students and instructors" (2013, 68). Marr aligns both the multiplicity of her oppression and her strategy for survival as being tied to that of her students' oppression and survival.

Many racialized women's voices are delegitimized through prevailing hierarchies and institutionalized methods of erasure, but my hope is that this book will serve as an intervention that further documents both the institutionalized reproduction of their inequity as well as their insistence on transforming the university and beyond. Even when opportunities to offer critical analysis have presented themselves, Black women who are contingent and often working class have been silenced even in the spaces that have been "created" for them.

I was forcefully reminded of this when I organized conference panels on two separate occasions in 2013 that featured the work of structurally and contractually contingent Black women—who, in the end, were unable to afford to attend either of the conferences. In both cases, the conference organizing committees accepted the women's abstracts, thus recognizing their scholarship as worthy contributions to their respective fields; but, as underresourced scholars, the women were ultimately deemed unsuitable as conference attendees because of their lack of financial resources. Academic conferences, even feminist ones that strive to keep race, class, and gender analysis at their center, are yet another institutionalized space whose market interests produce inequity for working-class academics, of which women of color are overrepresented. Yet, even with the publication of recent volumes that allude to women of color's mounting vulnerability within the restructured university, there is little critical attention given to how their actual economic and material conditions are produced and reproduced by the university and its counterparts. The lack of scholarship and activism surrounding these issues is both ironic and expected given the racialized shame, economic insecurity, and the pressure on academics to "perform" a middle-class status, regardless of the more likely working-class or poor realities facing many contingent scholars (Maisto 2013). In short, it is hardly surprising that there is a paucity of literature on highly educated, working-class Black women, given that those who would be most likely to write about these issues are precisely those facing the most barriers to academic writing and publication. The following section serves as a contribution to this history by focusing on the experiences of Black women who work as adjunct laborers.

Whose Academic Labor Movement?

Academic labor unions were developed, in part, to confront many of these labor conditions, yet the experiences of contingent faculty with academic unions has not been without controversy. This tension was evident in the current study. Most respondents saw the benefit of having union representation, yet those who were members of unions often reported feeling that their membership was of little consequence. They pointed out that their unions have not fully addressed the structural issues of race and gender that women of color academics confront. Trice noted:

> *I'm a little surprised that it's NOT more central to academic unions. . . . One of the guys I graduated from high school with is a regional director for SEIU [Service Employees International Union]. They definitely got that gender and diversity issues were important. I know a woman who works with the union to help get women into the trades now. She's an African American woman and definitely there's a piece of it where I'm fighting for the sisters. I don't see the academic unions as into that.*

As noted earlier, the American Federation of Teachers released two reports (2010, 2011) that suggest that gender and racial justice issues should be at the forefront of academic unions, but these issues were seldom included in the collective bargaining and union platforms with which these respondents have been affiliated. The women noted the material impact of paying union dues at a time when their pay is already meager. Trice expressed her frustration on this matter:

We do pay union dues. You can go to the union meetings. Do you receive information about the meetings? No. It's something you have to track yourself. I don't know when the meetings are; I just know I pay dues. I don't know my representatives. I don't know the president. I don't know anything besides the fact that I pay dues. When I went to the union, didn't really get any support. I thought, "This is just money coming out of my check to much of nothing."

She continued to reflect on her experience of seeking counsel from the unions in which she has been a member:

I'm going to be honest; I never got anything out of the union that was remotely helpful to me at either place. And I did run into some situations where I thought that the union should have been able to help me. I thought, "What does that mean if you're the union and you can't help me? Don't you see this as wrong?"

By failing to concern itself with issues that were relevant to her struggles as a racialized, gendered, and contingent body in the classroom, Trice's union organizations sent her a not-so-subtle message about whose interests it was really willing or meant to serve. Several other women expressed ambivalence regarding the point or benefit of organizing for better work conditions for contingent labor when what they actually hope for are permanent tenure-track positions with decent pay. They fear, not unreasonably, that organizing as adjuncts could inadvertently contribute to the normalization of that already proliferating labor category. Marquita discussed the adjuncts at her institution mobilizing after the death of former Duquesne adjunct faculty, Margaret Mary Vojtko:

So they were like "We're gonna start an adjunct committee." And I don't know how that went, but I was like "I'm not doin' that." [Laughs.] I just have too many other things going and I don't really know how long I'm gonna be adjuncting and I don't know how much of my life is gonna be given to that anymore. Now that I've been doing it for six years, I like the idea of teaching. I really like that, but it's very, very hard. You know like, always have to supplement that with something else and you're always just feeling very, very unsettled and unstable. And I was like "I don't want to join a committee and rally for that." [Laughs.] But I think that's important.

Several other women I interviewed had similar opinions, despite data that suggest institutions with unions have better work conditions than those without. As noted earlier, Black women are overrepresented not only as contingent laborers but also as academics who work in the South. Many respondents reside in southern states and therefore lacked access to academic unions. They were also paid at a lower rate than the national average for contingent faculty. This question of regional reach and impact connotes a departure from most academic labor discourse, which is usually centered on the recent momentum garnered by contingent faculty in the eastern, western, and midwestern regions of the United States.

Conclusion

The goal of this chapter has been to situate the knowledge economy's systemic and institutionalized forms of maintaining Black academic women's labor status in higher education through its reproduction of prevailing hierarchies embedded within its late-capitalist political economy. I argue that Black women face both *contractual* and *structural* forms of contingency in the twenty-first century. Naming and distinguishing between these two forms of contingency, as well as recognizing their disproportionate impact on women of color faculty is something that has, until recently, been largely absent from mainstream discussions critical of the university as a site of inequality. The two sections of the chapter are complementary in that I offer a reassessment of academic labor struggles that places Black women at the center and provides context by extending the history of academic contingency beyond contracts. I also create and demand a space where Black women who occupy both forms of contingency can offer their own analyses of the academy as multiply marginalized academic workers. In doing so, this chapter underscores the need to dismantle established hierarchies *among* academics—an issue often absent from current contingent labor discourse and struggles. Such discussions have not fully included the enduring difficulties of racialized workers, and even with the growing wave of gender analyses concerning the feminization of academic labor, there is virtually no description of how women academics are stratified by racial markers as well as contracts. Finally, this chapter is consistent with a long history of writings by women of color academics concerning their social justice orientations toward academic work. However, I also close with the caveat and warning to women of color academics to beware of efforts by the corporatized, neoliberal university to appropriate their voices and their very presence within the ivory tower in order to re-deploy them as evidence of the university's successful diversification. We need to refuse such efforts on the part of the university—with its slogans of promise, progress, and engagement—to market us against ourselves.

Chapter Three

Families Devalued: Black Academic Women and the Neoliberal Era's Family Tariff

First of all, it wasn't enough money. I didn't breast-feed, so she was on formula. I was getting $120 a month or something. The cans of formula were going every week, and they were $25.99, so the whole thing goes for formula. I didn't get WIC *and* [emphasis mine] food stamps; I just got the food stamps because I felt like WIC and food stamps was just too much for me. I was like, okay, I have to get social services, I have to get something. I need social services, fine. But I can't get *all* [emphasis mine] the social services. It was terrible to think like that. I just did not feel I should be doing it because I felt like white people feel; it's your choice that you're doing this job because you want to do it, as an adjunct. So you have to find a way to pay for yourself, or else people are going to start blaming you for staying in this job and taking all these resources from people. I don't know—it was just that same shame stuff. I was like, "I don't want to get on social services. I'm only going to pick the one." Well, actually two because she had to have insurance, so we were on Medicaid for prenatal care. That was already one. So I was like okay, food stamps, but I can't take WIC too. That will be everything, I'll be passing out. For black people, it's just that they are always associated with it. Regardless of their level of education.

—Marquita, adjunct professor

My pursuit of the dissertation led me to the social service line, after line, after line.

—Juhanna Nicole Rogers

One of the main arguments I make in this book is that Black academic women, a historically underrepresented group within the academy, are extremely vulnerable to hyperexploitation within the market-driven political economy of twenty-first-century higher education. Subsequently, highly educated Black women, like Marquita and Juhanna, who are also mothers attempting to "do what they love," often find themselves with more education, which has historically been touted as a buffer against poverty for people facing social disadvantage, but with less money, greater debt, food insecurity, no health care, and less child care than their male and white counterparts. More profoundly, Marquita described her inner turmoil and the internalized racism within her decision making, despite her economic and material need and even as she noted that obtaining aid was not enough to stabilize her family. She was very much aware that her anxieties were produced by broader racist and elitist messages concerning victim blaming of people who receive state support. Even the thought of needing multiple forms of support seemed to be too much for her to bear, in spite of her acknowledgment that her family would benefit from multiple forms of public assistance that she was economically qualified to receive.

In chapter 1, I positioned the corporate university as a producer of economic barriers that delay, prolong, and derail Black mothers' paths toward completion of graduate school as they face dwindling resources and skyrocketing educational costs. I note that Black women have persisted and are gaining more PhDs than ever, yet the narratives of precariously situated Black mother-academics suggest they are navigating neoliberal economic policies both inside and outside of higher education that negatively impact their educational and career progression. This chapter situates these compelling narratives against the backdrop of the enactment of liberal "family friendly" policies in higher education, the restriction of labor protections for contingent academic workers, and the specter of Clinton-era welfare reform policies. I argue that these forces are jointly contributing to the neoliberal cocktail that deepens Black academic mothers' and their families' inequity.

My findings suggest that instead of greater autonomy, the corporate university and a neoliberal US political and economic climate are producing highly educated Black mothers who must navigate an increased and often undesired reliance on heteronormative partnerships or the state in order to maintain their intellectual pursuits. Finally, from a Black feminist perspective, I explain the need for alternative models of understanding the intellectual persistence and resistance of one of the fastest-growing and most highly targeted populations in corporatized and privatized higher education: highly educated Black mothers.

Academic Mothers Navigating the Neoliberal University

Perhaps the time has come for academic women to stop colluding with a male system through their silence. . . . To be more open and communicative about the realities of being an academic mother, and to demand recognition of the differences which people bring with them to academic life are strategies which may help shatter the silence in which academic mothers are presently situated.

—Leonard & Malina (1994)

It is no secret that one of the greatest forms of institutionalized sexism faced by women in the labor force is the sheer lack of support they face if they are mothers or caregivers. The recent surge of anthologies and research focusing on women navigating and negotiating academic careers and mothering offer some insight on the barriers faced by this group of marginalized workers. Yet, the dominant discourse on academic mothering has primarily centered on work-life balance of tenure-track faculty or has focused on the manner in which tenure-track academic women must deftly negotiate their private lives within the gendered professional context of the academy (Bracken, Allen, & Dean 2006; Sullivan, Hollingshead, & Smith 2004). Almost annually, edited volumes offer much-needed analysis and testimony in the pursuit of shattering the silence surrounding academic mothers' existences within the academy. Yet these testimonies of gender inequity offer little class analysis, nor do they confront the economic vulnerability faced by working-class and less economically privileged women academics. In addition, these works also tend to offer little insight on how institutionalized racism within academia impacts academic women's, including mothers' career trajectories.

In response, many scholars have attempted to explain and address the stifling of academic mothers' careers, which many argue begins in graduate school. There is mounting evidence that there are gendered structural barriers such as "the leaking pipeline" and "maternal wall," which operate in ways that unjustly penalize academic women who mother. The "leaky pipeline" has been categorized as the widespread pattern of career disruption faced by many academic women, particularly those with young children, at every point of their professional path, and suggests that the male-centered culture of higher education has led to many women being forced out, down, or into the domestic sphere.

As a result, the University of California at Berkeley's *Creating a Family Friendly Department: Chairs and Deans Toolkit* (Frasch et al. 2007) was developed to offer guidelines to academic managers after years of Mary Ann Mason's research on the leaking pipeline phenomenon. Implementing family-friendly work policies helps in theory to decrease the leaks within the pipeline, yet tenure-track academic women remain timid about using maternity leave or tenure clock stoppage, given the gendered landscape of academic institutions. In addition, one of Joan Williams's focus group participants poignantly explained the machinations of racialized gender bias for structurally contingent women of color when she discussed navigating maternity leave: "I think gender biases work differently for women of different groups—race/ethnicity, immigration status, class of family of origin, and language. It's not just heightened for 'other' women. For example, the stereotype that women of certain groups have 'too many babies' affects perceptions of which women take time for family leave" (2012, 10).

Black academic women may not only face an economic and career penalty as a result of pregnancy and motherhood, but their sexuality and reproduction are at risk of being viewed through a racialized lens as well. The respondent's analysis above displays an awareness that women of color face particular scrutiny as subordinates within the realm of reproduction—a bias that travels with them into higher education institutions. In short, family policies in higher education seem to fail to take into account the well-documented history of backlash that Black women and other marginalized women are already facing, regardless of their caregiving status. That must be confronted in addition to gender equity and other social justice issues.

In the previous chapter, I also noted that academic women, regardless of institutional makeup, are precariously employed disproportionately and have little access to the family-friendly options proposed by gender equity advocates. Mary Ann Mason and her colleagues (2006) accurately note the massive loss of mother academics into the contingent labor force, but their recommendations and policies are generally designed to support tenure-track faculty. Interventions intended to support tenure-track women do not adequately address labor reform, which may have a more significant impact on academic mothers given that contingent labor has been feminized and normalized. Family-friendly polices also do not serve to dismantle the stratified hierarchies among academic women that are maintained when gender inequity is confronted in isolation from other interactive forms of inequity, such as racism, contract status, wage inequity, health care benefits, and job security that would help academic mothers more broadly.

Similar to the "leaking pipeline," the concept of "the maternal wall" has been used to define the economic and professional ghettos that academic women face once they become mothers (Crosby, Williams, & Biernat 2004). The maternal wall suggests that gendered workplace barriers are mobilized against working mothers because an unresolvable contradiction stands between the expectation of the ideal (masculine/disembodied/objective/rational) worker and the expectation of the ideal (feminine/embodied/subjective/emotional) mother. Indeed, rank-and-file workers, including academics, often are forced to suppress their interpersonal connections to families and communities, as well as any other evidence of their corporeal existence, in order to be touted as "ideal workers" within capitalist, rational, economic models of productivity (Chan & Fisher 2008). However, the notion of the maternal wall has generally been conceptualized and researched independent of academic women's widely divergent social locations.

For instance, although Black women's working conditions within the academy involve context-specific challenges, working outside the home is a familiar role for many Black women and Black mothers. Thus, Black academic women who choose to become mothers embody an axis of contradiction within the binary of the "ideal worker/ideal mother" framework used by most scholars who study academic motherhood. The metaphor of the "ideal worker" narrowly considers gender exclusive of its interaction with race, class, and other social factors. Black women's reproductive and labor experiences have never had the privilege of being dichotomized in these ways. In addition, Patricia Hill Collins also has suggested that economic providing has historically been part of Black women's conceptions of "good mothering" (Collins 1987, 49). This view serves as a counterpoint to Crosby, Williams, & Biernat's (2004) conceptualization of the "ideal mother" and "ideal worker" binary, because Black feminist notions of good mothering have been theorized as being congruent with economic provision for many Black women who are both mothers and workers.

The rise in "maternal wall"–based discrimination litigation among academic women also evidences a disturbing nuanced trend in gender-based discrimination within the workplace (AAUW 2004, 1). Current data suggest that only 6 percent of discrimination cases are brought to trial, and only one-third of them are won on the basis of race, ethnicity, disability, or gender (Nielsen, Nelson, & Lancaster 2010, 175–201); however, pregnancy discrimination cases have a significantly higher success rate of 50 percent (AAUW 2004, 9). This trend in litigation runs the risk of privileging women who articulate pregnancy and motherhood as the sole issue in their discrimination and potentially undermines any intersectional discrimination claims that might be put forth by women of color who are pregnant and/or mothers/caregivers. Collectively, these issues, histories, and sociocultural understandings outline a series of interactive barriers that Black women and other women of color face upon entry into the academy. It behooves us, then, to examine Black women's decisions, choices, and their journeys as academic mothers within this context.

A broader approach to support the working lives of contingent academic mothers is especially important given the rise of non-tenure-track appointments over the past two decades, as well as for graduate student mothers, given the surge of women now earning PhDs (see appendix B for resources). Black women's overrepresentation as structurally and contractually contingent laborers, as noted in chapter 2, makes them less likely to benefit from the purported gender equity initiatives implemented by universities. In addition, gender-only analysis and intervention that fail to consider the racialization of women of color are unable to adequately capture their needs.

Women academics with caregiving responsibilities are generally positioned to "choose" part-time academic work more often than men because it is framed as "more flexible" and "family friendly," yet research reveals that the intensified demands of the restructured corporatized university continue to encroach on personal time and resources through the blurred boundaries of online teaching, larger class sizes, and less centralized work locations—all of which impact women of color and mothering academics disproportionately. These rhetorical strategies fit perfectly with a neoliberal and individualist landscape of the university. Those women who "hang on" to doing what they love most often cobble together adjunct positions or acquire academic staff positions that serve the needs of the institution at the expense of their own lives and professional goals. Some may continue to serve the very institutions that have consistently limited their full access.

Thus the implementation of family-friendly policies has served as a weak, liberal, feminist intervention within the late-capitalist political economy and elite work culture of the university and does not address the established hierarchies among academic women.

Feminist Critiques of Academic Mothering in the Neoliberal University

Feminist scholars have offered analyses that extend beyond theories of gender equity and instead locate the mother-academic as a subject within the neoliberal university and the larger society. Together they provide an excellent beginning for framing the narratives captured in this book. Lynn O'Brien Hallstein and Andrea O'Reilly (2012) assert that as feminists we must keep a steady eye on the alleged gains of second-wave feminist struggles for gender equity in the workplace. They offer a compelling argument for examining contemporary academic mothers' circumstances as representative of the conflict between the unbounded work expectations of the contemporary, corporatized academy and the unbounded expectations of twenty-first-century intensive mothering.

In addition to the expectation of *intensive mothering* outlined by O'Brien Hallstein and O'Reilly, many Black women, other women of color, and working-class academic women are simultaneously facing the realities of *extensive mothering*. This theory considers both the intersectional contours of women of color's mothering experiences in relation to their work experiences as marginalized academics within a historically racialized, patriarchal, antifamily, individualist, and increasingly marketized professional context. Extending the boundaries of academic motherhood captures the breadth and depth of maternal practices performed by Black women within and outside of the academy. This hybridized construction of mothering complicates Laurel Thatcher Ulrich's early dichoto-mization of intensive/extensive mothering (1982), by offering a contemporary interpretation of "mothering" to best capture the scope and impact of Black women's maternal performances and labor. In addition to mothering their own children in the context of a late-capitalist, patriarchal, and racialized society, they are also expected to perform mothering and care work to a wide swath of others, owing to structural inequities both within and outside of the academy. This expansive net of maternal practices for many academic women of color encompasses the sociopolitical interventions undergirding much of their intel-lectual work and academic labor practices and coexists with the pressures of the newest racialized and privileged measuring stick of intensive mothering.

Thus far, the omission of the complexities, expansive scope, and locations of women of color academics' extensive moth-ering has at times rendered their experiences further invisible in the current bio-legal mothering discourse, the separate spheres discourse, as well as the privileged location of aca-demic mothering on the tenure track. We must demand more comprehensive responses from institutions, researchers, and policymakers who are currently considering single-issue solu-tions that center on gender equity interventions while re-maining silent on mutually constitutive social justice issues such as race, class, and faculty hierarchies.

Sara Motta's two essays, "And Still We Rise: On the Violence of Marketisation in Higher Education" and "The Messiness of Motherhood in the Marketised University" (both 2012), focus on the violence of the marketized academy. Motta notes the "competing demands" of both institutions, as advanced by O'Brien Hallstein and O'Reilly (2012) but discusses mother-hood and care work as being intensified because of the "col-lapse and/or privatization of welfare provision." This departure from the class privilege discourse that defines intensified forms of mothering more keenly positions the reality of women of color, adjunct, student, and other working-class academic mothers. Motta notes that the culture of higher education pairs well with neoliberal subjectivity in that both conditions impose order, discipline, and a divorce from the lived experience. Yet she describes motherhood in the marketized academy as messy and ill-fitting for the individualist, capitalist, disembodied place and space of higher education and as a place of resistance.

Motta also suggests that both the marketized space and time of academia corrupt and impose unnamed burdens upon motherhood, although the converse is disallowed. She argues that this violence of denial of self and relationship attempts to "eradicate spaces and times of possibility and with this, criminalize and erase forms of being, acting and thinking outside of commodified logics" (2012, 2).

The By-Products of Doing What You Love: Highly Educated Black Mothers and the Production of Economic Need

And they were like, "Send us your pay stub from your adjuncting job, and we'll reassess and give you food stamps again."

—Marquita

This section positions the neoliberal university as a site where the "doing what you love" aspirations of highly educated women of color are replaced by basic survival, thus pointing to the spurious relationship between education and class for women of color in the twenty first century. The women in this study are all talented scholars and educators who sacrificed a great deal to earn their graduate degrees and continue their careers as professors. The leaking pipeline theory suggests that many women—particularly mothers—are lost somewhere along the academic trajectory, but how do those who remain hang on? As the academic workforce has become more casualized, several trends have emerged for non-elite academic women as they continue their intellectual pursuits. Since they are severely underpaid, there are limited economically viable opportunities for them to pursue their careers, especially if they have dependents.

Higher education historically has been viewed as socially and economically beneficial for all groups of women, yet the cumulative effects of widespread defunding and privatization of higher education, as well as the rising cost and expansion of undergraduate, graduate, and professional degree and certificate programs, are not only diminishing but also defining the educational careers and economic prospects for many aspiring Black academic women who are mothers or caregivers. For example, some parents interested in college are deterred because the cost of a college education is prohibitive, while other college-educated parents face compounded barriers because they are already debt-burdened from their undergraduate studies and would require financial and material support to care for their families and focus on their advanced educational endeavors.

In addition, the neoliberal practices of casualizing and feminizing the faculty have essentially assured that non-elite academics' families are increasingly subsidized by the state. UC Berkeley's Center for Labor Research and Education (Jacobs, Perry, & MacGillvary 2015) reported that almost a quarter of all contingent professors are receiving some form of public assistance. These deteriorating economic conditions are a cause for concern for all academics, but they also shed light on the spurious relationship between education, race, and class for women of color in the twenty-first century. For example, Juhanna Nicole Rogers, a PhD candidate and mother of a young child, penned an essay sharing her testimony about the material conditions she faced as a Black woman PhD student as she confronted multiple funding barriers and the lived paradox of conducting research on similar topics concerning the intersections of race, class, and gender. Rogers reveals the critical need many self-funded graduate students have for basic survival resources like food, and the role the state plays in granting aid to underresourced graduate students:

I received the news that my financial aid limit has been reached one week before starting my final year. Life as I knew it changed. My plan—so well thought out and meticulous—was derailed. Instead of one with assistance with devoted time to write, I took on an additional teaching load and a part-time job to cover expenses. The more I worked, the further away my writing became. Working three jobs and trying to write a dissertation is a tragedy waiting to happen. In order to complete my dissertation, I should have been in the library reading, writing and editing. Writing a dissertation requires a critical level of focus and discipline, all which I quickly lost. On top of this, I also had to fulfill my motherly duties. Needless to say, finding reserve mental space and energy was more than a challenge. I lost steam. And with pockets full of lint, I had to visit the public assistance office—one of many visits, I'd soon find out. (Rogers 2015)

The online comments to her essay, which appeared on For Harriet, a journalistic website that publishes social and political content relevant to Black women, vacillated between cheering her on toward the finish line and commiserating with and recognizing the reality that she portrays. Rogers, like several of the women I interviewed, describes hunger and reliance on state aid as conditions produced *by* their graduate school experience. Several of the women I interviewed were fortunate to have spouses and extended family members who could help to supply them and their families with groceries and meals, but others spoke of needing to rely on public assistance and charity in order to survive. Still for others, the thought of relying on public assistance was perceived as too much to bear. Facing the need for financial support in the midst of their graduate education or adjunct employment, these women were forced, painfully and paradoxically, to navigate the powerful racialized and gendered stereotype of the "welfare queen" even as they were taking steps to actively counter such vitriol.

The Welfare Queen Goes to College?!

The tensions between needing public assistance and utilizing it can be a racialized and gendered minefield for Black women, and highly educated Black women are no exception. As the subjects of widespread racialized and gendered accusations of laziness and fraudulence, several respondents found it difficult to acquire the support their families needed. Some were so vicariously traumatized by stigmatization that they chose not to take or limit their reliance on much needed public assistance. Marquita proudly stated, "I just couldn't do it. I took the food stamps, but I couldn't take the WIC, too." She noted that she qualified for both and was uncomfortable when others recommended that she seek such aid when she became a mother. When asked why she would not use the aid available to her, she replied, "I just couldn't." Her comments reflect the personal shame and general discomfort related to needing support as a highly educated Black woman. When asked whether she was receiving state-sponsored support, Niyah, a doctoral candidate responded, ". . . yes, but I will only use them for a little while." The added qualification here speaks to both Marquita's and Niyah's resistance to the burden of being labeled as state dependent and their empowered stance to claim a better position in life, even when all conditions are stacked against them.

Many contingent faculty face economic crises during the summer months, when they essentially become unemployed. Marquita noted that ideas associated with Black people's connection to welfare drove her distaste for using public assistance during a time of economic instability. She reflected on how needing help made her feel, especially when she thought she was being associated with welfare because she was a Black single mother.

> It was summer, so I didn't have any income, and it was really hard. I tried to save up enough money for the entire summer so we wouldn't be so tight. It got really tight. He [a friend] was telling me, "You can apply for those." "You have a kid. You can get these services!" I was like, first of all, I didn't want to take them because I'd had them before and I knew how that felt. But I also didn't like having it suggested to me, either, you know? Like, "You're exactly the type of person who qualifies." It was like, "You're hungry, you're poor, and you're black." All of those things were true. I am poor and hungry, but I also have the ability to earn more money, and I just feel like I need to exercise that ability more and stay off food stamps. I just didn't want to be on them.

A similar racialized sentiment was revealed in the 2012 *Chronicle of Higher Education* exposé, "The PhD Now Comes with Food Stamps." Staff writer Stacey Patton interviewed Melissa Bruninga-Matteau, a white, 43-year-old single mother with a PhD, who felt compelled to begin her interview by stating, "I am not a welfare queen." Patton reports that Bruninga-Matteau says the stereotype of the people receiving such aid does not reflect reality. While Bruninga-Matteau is attempting to assert the actual diversity of those who receive state assistance, she also conveys a need to distance herself from poor Black women, the implicitly understood population *expected* to receive public assistance. Patton also interviewed Keisha Hawkins-Sledge, who at the time was a PhD candidate and mother of two. Hawkins-Sledge reflected on the burden of others' racialized and gendered gaze: "My name is Keisha. You hear that name and you think black girl, big hoop earrings, on welfare, three or four babies' daddies," she says. "I had to work against my color, my flesh, and my name alone. I went to school to get all these degrees to prove to the rest of the world that I'm not lazy and I'm not on welfare. But there I was and I asked myself, 'What's the point? I'm here anyway.'" Like Hawkins-Sledge's sentiments, themes of despair echoed throughout many of my interviews as participants realized that, regardless of their education and hard work—and indeed, *because of it*, they were experiencing additional economic burdens and social scrutiny. Marquita tried to capture what she defined as "the calculus of poverty" in explaining all the things that one must be mathematically savvy about in order to demonstrate need:

> *The food stamps supplement, the low income, the money that you have to pay for rent, the other expenses for your child or your children. So you need them. But if you work twice as hard to get off them, then you still can't afford food. It's a weird sort of chess that you have to play. It's a calculus of poverty, and you have to be really, really good at navigating things that you don't really understand. I didn't really want to be part of that because I'm horrible at budgeting and math.*

On the other hand, some participants did not see the use of public assistance from a place of shame but rather as a forced choice, particularly if they were in graduate school. Alexis explained:

They require for individuals to come in, and they only give you a sti-pend of $430 a month, and my rent is double that. I know that I need that and if I didn't have that, then I would be busting my butt to try to find other resources or find another stream of income so that I would be able to meet my needs. I don't really like it, but I see it as a stepping-stone. As I'm stepping up the ladder, these are the things that I need, and it's available to me; so I'm going to take advantage of it and do what's necessary to do. Now if there's anything that I can do to get around it, then I will. But if I can't, I just have to keep going.

She also elaborated on her resolve and determined thinking as she drifted away from economic independence while moving toward more education:

I think originally I had concerns about being on public assistance when taking my graduate education. I felt uncomfortable because I've never been . . . my mother has received benefits of social service, but as long as I can remember I've held a job. I've been technically working since the age of nine. So I've always had income, and I've always been that go-to person. If somebody needs money for this bill or that bill, I've always had the finance to be able to provide for myself and for others. So then when I'm at a place where I'm not able to provide for myself or for others, and I'm on the receiving end, I think it's done something to my social standing and my confidence. I think it led me into a state of depression in thinking, "Can I do this?" But after I changed my perception, I realized, "Okay, this is only tempo-rary. If you're on the opposite end, it's okay, because there's a lesson to be learned from all of this."

Alexis feels that her use of social services will only be temporary, and her optimism reflects her drive to maneuver beyond her present circumstances. Yet, the current economic climate in the United States suggests that as increasing numbers of highly educated Americans face ballooning educational debt and underemployment, they are finding themselves in need of more support to make ends meet. The rise in debt has lowered the real income of middle-class Americans, and those who must maintain households, who face other forms of structural racism and sexism, and who have families are particularly vulnerable.

An End to Welfare as We Need It

The most recent welfare reform in the United States was initiated in 1996, when President Clinton signed the Personal Responsibility and Work Opportunity Reconciliation Act and declared that "welfare as we know it" had ended. This legislation instituted the Temporary Assistance for Needy Families program (TANF), effectively replacing the 61-year-old federal assistance program called Aid to Families with Dependent Children (AFDC). While this and earlier family support programs were designed primarily to help households headed by widowed white women after World War I, the civil rights legislation of the 1960s increased federal investment in poverty reduction programs, which allowed more low-income women of color to apply for and receive AFDC benefits. This shift in policy focus changed public attitudes, and political rhetoric became increasingly gendered, racialized, elitist, and laced with vitriol (Gilens 1999; Neubeck & Cazenave 2001).

TANF included several new requirements, including a greater emphasis on marriage, strict time limits for program participation, and a preference for paid work over education, thus severely limiting routes to higher education. Specifically, low-income mothers are expected to work outside the home in exchange for cash benefits, food assistance, access to child care, and other forms of aid. These conditions altered the early AFDC program from one that entitled poor families to access to resources needed to sustain their families to one in which the beneficiaries had to meet a strict set of conditions in labor market participation in order to receive much-needed resources to keep families economically stable. Specifically, the push for changes to welfare law served as a coordinated attack against already vulnerable family systems in poor communities.

US policymakers continue to communicate that paid work is simply a more pressing concern for low-income mothers than education. For instance, the US Department of Health and Human Services published guidelines in June 2006 initially stating that attending college to pursue a bachelor's or master's degree was to be eliminated from the educational options that parents receiving TANF could choose from in order to satisfy program requirements. Restrictions on enrolling in doctoral programs were not mentioned—possibly because less of the population was actively pursuing them and because the achievement orientations and intellectual capacities of poor women and women of color are minimized.

These proposed modifications of the 1996 policy clarified that TANF "was not intended to be a college scholarship program" (US Department of Health and Human Services 2006, 37460), yet the department eventually published a revised version of the guidelines, where these proposed educational restrictions were retracted. The policy language was made to be flexible and allowed states discretion in defining local social service, but the underlying message communicated by federal lawmakers is that job attainment ought to take precedence over pursuing a postsecondary degree. Specifically, many states place limits on college program choice and the number of months for which TANF participants can attend college. Brianna described her struggle to navigate public assistance in Maryland as a mother in graduate school:

> For individuals that are trying to step outside of their background and trying to advance, they're penalized because they're not eligible for programs that are necessary for their advancement. I guess that's basically what I was trying to say as far as me trying to get a graduate degree and not being eligible for certain programs because the requirements say that you have to have a bachelor's degree and only a bachelor's degree. But there are exceptions to most rules, and the exception is if you're in a program, the days that you're in the program they will give you child care. But the days you're not in the program, then you have to pay for child care. So I was forced to pay for two days or something like that for child care. This was in the job training program. So they supplied me with child care when I was in job training, but no child care when I was in graduate school.

In addition, in many states, those who receive child care assistance through TANF have to be employed for a minimum of 20 hours a week. This work must be paid work and often does not include the independent research, writing, and other modes of intellectual work that many graduate students are completing. Some states count educational activities as work but mandate that TANF participants must be in class a minimum of 10 hours a week and be enrolled in a program from which they could graduate within 24 months. These conditions are typically not applicable to graduate and professional students, given that most take between four and six years to complete advanced graduate programs. In fact, the American Institutes for Research (2013) found that Black PhD students in STEM fields, who are most often underfunded and facing institutional and societal barriers, are more likely take 7 to 10 years to complete their doctoral degrees.

Brianna elaborated and shared the ways in which she must navigate the system as a graduate student mother:

I was told to apply for temporary cash assistance, which is a program that provides cash to individuals with children. I was told to apply for this program, then they boost you up on the list and they have to give you child care. But you go through a job training program; you have to look for a job weekly. And you have to be there Monday through Friday from 8 to 4. So I had to do this in order to get the child care.

Fiona Pearson argues that "many . . . policy makers have tended to downplay the correlation between education and income, emphasizing instead the importance of mothers securing a job" (2007, 723). In February 2018, Pearson testified before Connecticut's Higher Education Subcommittee of the Appropriations Committee and presented data from the Institute on Women's Policy Research (Noll, Reichlin, and Gault 2017) that revealed 26 percent of undergraduates are student parents; 71 percent of those student parents are women; 43 percent of all undergraduate student parents are single mothers; and that in 2011, 47 percent of Black women students, 32 percent of Latina or Hispanic women students, and 29 percent of white women students were parents. Her testimony aimed to help the state legislators of Connecticut understand how welfare reforms, which restrict educational opportunities, are disproportionately affecting already underresourced segments of Connecticut's population, but her remarks have implications well beyond the conditions within her state. Higher education is considered one of the few avenues by which women who are mothers can attain greater economic sufficiency, yet the high cost of college coupled with restrictive TANF policies are now jointly limiting access to college, graduate school, and careers for many African American women throughout the United States and are exacerbating the conditions in which poverty is produced.

The ideological and political decisions of the 1996 welfare-to-work reforms that created restrictions in TANF continue to have reverberations in policy decisions for low-income families today. Several of this study's participants shared that they and their families have experienced hunger and food insecurity. The need for benefits from the Supplemental Nutrition Assistance Program (SNAP), formerly referred to as food stamps, signifies hunger and food insecurity is becoming particularly pronounced for those seeking or with an advanced education as they navigate educational debt and low wages (Patton 2012). The number of Americans with a graduate education, either master's or doctorate, who receive SNAP nearly tripled between 2007 and 2010. Specifically, the number of people with master's degrees who received food stamp benefits jumped from 101,682 to 293,029 within that three-year period. Additionally, among people with doctorates, the receipt of federal food benefits increased from 9,776 to 33,655. Though these numbers pale in comparison with the general population, what is most concerning is the drastic increase within such a short period of time.

Despite increased need for food for many US families, the 2020 federal SNAP guidelines have increased barriers and confusion for low-income college student parents in need of nutritional support. The Trump administration's new rule also limits states' ability to waive the requirement that able-bodied adults must participate in paid work at least 20 hours a week in order to receive their SNAP benefits. These changes negatively impact over 700,000 SNAP recipients, including graduate and professional student parents who increasingly cannot afford basic living expenses like food (Treisman 2019). The participants in the current study, some graduate students and some professors, exemplify the great need for food support in stark contrast to the current administration's decisions about who deserves to have access to US taxpayer resources.

During our one-on-one interviews, when I asked participants whether they and/or their families had experienced hunger during their studies, responses were pained but forthright. For instance, Alexis responded, "I have, they haven't," disclosing her sacrifice of food for her children's sake. Brianna acknowledged, "No, we haven't gone hungry, but we have been very close. I would say I'm close to that position now." Similarly, Niyah shared, "We never went hungry because we always had enough, but it has been close." Both hunger and the threat of hunger are part of their self-defined sense of precariousness produced by multiple years of graduate study, underfunding, and low wages.

As further evidence of the increase of economic strain and hunger faced by graduate students in this historical moment, we can also note the steady increase of student food banks at many US colleges and universities. Undergraduates and graduate students, as well as faculty, have all benefited from them. Michigan State University's Student Food Bank is the oldest established student food bank in the United States, and a quick scan of its webpage reveals testimonies exclusively from economically struggling graduate students who are grateful to have this level of material support. While Michigan State's food bank is 20 years old, there have been 76 food banks founded on campuses across the United States in recent years. Yet the emergence of education-induced economic crises, which are steeped in histories of gendered racism, simultaneously puts women of color and poor women in a position of often needing to hide their reality and need for support (Adair & Dahlberg 2003).

Juhanna Nicole Rogers further explicates her desperation for food and survival as a doctoral student: "This was my fifth visit in nine days, so I had hope that this would be the day that

I was approved for food assistance. We were down to our last few dollars and were in need of groceries. I could go without, but my son couldn't." Rogers's desperation to care for her family while simultaneously attempting to complete her degree is evident.

In addition to food insecurity noted by Rogers, Alexis, a participant in the current study, shared that housing and utilities are often crisis-level concerns for her family as she tries to complete her graduate degree. She, too, needed the support of local human service agencies to stay afloat:

> I went to Salvation Army. So that prevented me from getting evicted that time. As far as utilities go, I applied for energy assistance. I applied in October of 2012. I had not paid my light bill because I was waiting for the energy assistance. They did not pay the assistance until June of 2013. So in May of 2013, it was to the point they said, "Okay, you maxed out all your assistance. If you don't pay your bill, your lights will be disconnected this day!"

Alexis also reflected on her discomfort with and reliance on public assistance that was a condition of her graduate school experience:

> Originally I felt uncomfortable because I've never been ... my mother has received benefits of social service, but as long as I can remember I've held a job. So this is that different thing that I've had to go through and rely on the system, but it's not gonna be for the rest of my life. I understand that and I realize, what they have, I need and I'll have to do what it is that they require me to do as long as I need it to work. It's funny. Because I had a graduate degree, it's almost like there are things coming at me to push me back.

The need for formal support for parents both within and outside of higher education is apparent, even when it was coupled with shame. The testimonials of this study's participants also revealed the ways in which US social policies that are meant to respond to the material and economic needs of families are often the barriers to their success.

In addition to TANF restrictions for college-bound participants, the context in which TANF is administered is important. Fiona Pearson notes that "case managers' discretionary support varied widely, in part because of the pressure they experienced from upper-level administrators to reduce caseloads and increase the number of clients working paid jobs" (2007, 725). Marquita mentioned the level of surveillance and distrust she felt from public assistance workers: "They are so far into your business with that, all these questionnaires, all these things, they talk to you terribly, so condescending, 'Have you looked for work? Are you sure?' And you prove it. Nobody believes you."

College student TANF participants, particularly those at the graduate level like Marquita and others in the current study, require the support of their case managers. Alexis also shared experiences that she interpreted as uncooperative and hostile treatment from workers:

> I've had several workers say to me, "Why aren't you working or why don't you have a job?" They don't understand the demands of the program and my specific situation and all the circumstances that are involved. It's almost like there are things coming at me to push me back. And maybe this is only how I feel. When I say they push me back, I feel like, "We really don't want you in the program anyway. So you need to make sure you're doing exactly everything and we're not going to make any other exceptions for you. But you make the smallest mistake and we're kicking you out." I just felt like they have tried to put me out of the program.

Finally, proponents of welfare reform have argued that as more poor mothers enter the workforce, they will be able to benefit from labor market safety nets such as unemployment insurance. Unemployment insurance was created in 1935 to help workers and their families and to "play a key role in helping businesses, communities, and the nation's economy. Since then, the program has continued to help cushion the impact of economic downturns and bring economic stability to communities, states, and the nation by providing temporary income support for laid-off workers" (US Department of Labor 2019). However, data suggest that those who moved off the welfare rolls did not fare better once they lost employment and began to draw unemployment. In fact, unemployment insurance, like TANF, has posed additional restrictions for poor and working-class academics. Many are precariously employed by colleges and universities, falling between the cracks regarding the definition of unemployment. As such, they often cannot collect the insurance to stabilize their families during economic crises. The New Faculty Majority, an organization fighting for rights for contingent faculty, has launched a campaign to track this trend. Wanda Evans-Brewer, whom we met at the beginning of chapter 2, faced this paradox firsthand. She explained how she is being sued for fraud by the state of Illinois for attempting to receive unemployment during times when she has not been given a course and is in practice "essentially" unemployed. Yet the state of Illinois claims that while Evans-Brewer is subsisting in employment purgatory, she is not unemployed and is demanding that she repay $400 per week. She reported not having the funds to comply, so the state has begun the process of garnisheeing her federal income tax refund. The university she was adjuncting for can be viewed as complicit in criminalizing its contingent faculty because it refused to draft a letter of clarification explaining the flexible nature of Wanda's employment contract and the precariousness of her employment. Doing so would further expose its destabilization and manipulation of her employment and income. Though the respondents in the current study noted the failures of systems that they thought were designed to support them, many also shared the ways in which informal support systems were often the stabilizing forces in their lives.

Black Academic Women Navigating Heteronormativity

When I was adjuncting I was always stressed because I'm a very proud person. Even though I'm married, I like economic independence, and it was very, very stressful for me to have to rely on my husband so much.

—Charli, adjunct professor

While some graduate student and adjunct mothers navigated what Marquita referred to as the "calculus of poverty" by searching for support from the state, others discussed the economic protections they received or were expected to receive from their male partners or children's fathers. Alexis, who was a single mother, was penalized by welfare workers who denied her child care benefits because the nature of her co-parenting relationship with her child's father exists outside the definition of formal economic dependence.

Currently I receive temporary cash assistance, medical assistance, food stamps, and child care is kinda up in the air right now because they took it from me because they said I wasn't complying with the child support. But hopefully they're giving it back within the next month or so. I wasn't compliant because they said that I needed to give them the original court documents from the state of Illinois, which I did not have. I contacted the state of Illinois; they then failed to send them over to them. So since they didn't have the papers in their hand that they needed, I wasn't compliant. Regardless of what Illinois failed to do, it all falls back on me. And me not providing them with what it is that they need. My daughter is currently in Illinois for the summer. She will be back in a week. So that's how I was able to get around that, and that's why I say her father does act as a support, but he's there and he can only do so much because he's not working. He had a business, but now his business is closed because it wasn't doing well. Now he has no income, but he does keep my child. So she is there with him.

While Alexis's co-parenting arrangement appears to be amicable while she attends graduate school in the summer, it evokes a particular reminder that mothers and their children are supposed to be economically dependent upon men, not the state. She was "punished" by taking away her child care. Heteronormative dependence reverberated through the interviews as other participants discussed the multitude of ways it was imposed upon them while they tried to navigate their educational and professional lives.

Marquita, a longtime adjunct who had to look elsewhere for income after becoming a mother, described the contemporary adjunct as someone who could afford to be a part-time worker. To her, adjuncting is becoming a space of heteronormative privilege, one which she defined as being more compatible with white women's circumstances. She reflected:

Interestingly, I find that adjuncting works for married people, like someone who has a partner who earns [in] an entirely different field and they earn a lot more, you know, so you can get on their health care, you can get on their maintaining most of the bills. I know a lot of women like that at this school, and I have known them at other schools too. If you have a partner who will carry you, so to speak, financially that's pretty much how people wind up in these careers for a long time.

She continued, "And a lot of the people who are non-Black are privileged in some way. Married, or this is their second job, or they work there full-time." She recalled the lack of resources when there is no partner to depend on:

I've never had health benefits, and they don't offer maternity leave to adjuncts at all. Sometimes they will offer health benefits, but I've never been eligible for them. I think you have to teach there for like three years and then they'll let you enroll, but they take like a big chunk out of your adjunct pay. So a lot of people just opt not to do it and they like get on their partner's insurance.

The notion that hetero-marital privilege is viewed as a stabilizing factor in academic women's economic status emerges throughout my interviews in this study. Many of the women were navigating the felt or real economic reliance on male partners as their educational debt increased and/or their employment opportunities were truncated. Their narratives concerning dependence on husbands/partners in order to be an academic reflected positive feelings of support, gratitude, and relief, as well as the negative feelings previously described by Charli, concerning of shame, loss of pride, and guilt for being dependent on others. Economic dependence on male partners ranged from additional income to the provision of day care and health insurance. Annisha shared how being married was helpful to her ability to secure child care. "Yes, I was able to have affordable child care because I had a child, and then I got married. So that was such a blessing." And then she elaborated, "I am married. Thank the Lord that I'm married! I don't know how single people in this environment where you're getting paid $1,500/class per semester, I don't know how single people do it. I'm married and my husband is a wonderful man, very understanding. He basically covers me."

Additionally, Charli shared, "Yes, I have been without health insurance. This is before I got married." Over and over, the Black academic women explained how their hetero relationships with men protect them from economic insecurity. Trice disclosed, "One of the things that happened, fortunately I married my husband, tenured, so we're fine along those lines. But the reality of health issues. I know it's going to catch up to me because I haven't been in a full-time position for about ten years. I got sick, so I had about four surgeries and I thought to myself, 'If my husband wasn't there, what would have happened?'"

Instead of greater economic autonomy, the burden of educational debt coupled with less-than-ideal academic labor has produced dependency. However, heteronormativity is not always coupled with economic privilege for racialized groups. Black men in the United States are disproportionately underemployed and face similar labor market discrimination. Thus the Black women they are partnered with and the children they are responsible for are not always protected economically. Niyah, an adjunct, doctoral candidate, and married mother of two shared how her family of four cobbles together health care:

> We belong to a nonprofit health center, so it's income-based. It's run by a Christian organization, so that's where we go for health care. We can see a doctor, a therapist, and dentist, OBGYN. They have basic medical services, and its income-based, so you pay based on your income. As long as you're working, then you qualify for care there. Our kids, of course, are covered through the state health insurance program for children. They were also covered that way in Texas. When we moved here, that's when we went to the church health care center.

Trice, despite being married to a man who is a tenured professor, admitted that even his income could not protect her from the educational debt that she has accrued. She declared in a defeated tone, "Because our finances were so screwed up between all these educational pieces that we would never qualify for a mortgage. With the bankruptcy, we would never qualify for a loan for a house."

Conclusion

During our time together, Wanda Evans-Brewer shared that she no longer is interested in being hired as a full-time, tenure-track professor, although she loves teaching and writing. She decided to share her story and expose the practices of the university so that the next generation of graduate students and professors may benefit. Her struggle, her resilience, and her survival are evident, but the violence the university is inflicting upon its people, particularly Black women, is often hidden in plain sight.

The neoliberal decisions to limit educational funding, pay academic workers poorly, and increase the costs of tuition suggest that broad-based reform is necessary not only for students entering higher education but also for graduate students and faculty who are already there. The voices in this book help us to see that family, friends, professors, and understanding case managers have helped to keep them above water. Yet, this age-old pattern of community-based support cannot be the official model for sustaining parents who are students or contingent faculty.

I echo Fiona Pearson's contention that "support from prevailing social institutions is necessary if low-income mothers are to be provided with postsecondary educational access" (Pearson 2007, 229). These supports have drastically waned in the twenty-first century and are not only reproducing old forms of inequity that deny students access; they are also producing new forms of inequity by setting up both an ironic and worrisome scenario for highly educated faculty and graduate students who find themselves in the welfare line.

We must demand more comprehensive responses from institutions, researchers, and policymakers who are currently considering single-issue solutions that center on gender equity interventions while remaining silent on mutually constitutive social justice issues such as racism, classism, labor exploitation, and institutionalized hierarchies. These are critical points of engagement and praxis for feminists and academic labor activists who are committed to transforming exploitative social institutions into equitable ones.

Chapter Four

Jumping Mountains: Resisting the Marketized University

> I want to prepare you. When you leave my classroom, I want you to be a critical thinker. Think about your world. Not only do I want you to think about your world but make the right applications. In addition to being a great writer, be able to communicate in writing. I want my students to always think about their world. Always think critically. We have too much non-thinking in this country as is!
>
> —Charli, adjunct professor

Throughout this book, I have documented the institutionalized and market-driven barriers confronting highly educated, professionally committed Black women who struggle, scrape by, and persist within higher education institutions. I intentionally applied a *woman of color feminist critique of higher education* to examine the collateral effects of Black academic women's experiences of inequity, which I have argued are hyperproduced under increasingly corporatized practices and policies in higher education in the neoliberal era. The preceding chapters have illustrated what Jeffrey Williams has defined as "neoliberalism in action" in higher education and shed light on the by-products of late-capitalist practices by mapping the complex educational and professional lives of precariously situated Black academic women.

In this fourth chapter I shift my lens of analysis to foreground the insights and analyses of these very same Black academic women, who despite having to navigate these economic and institutional conditions, offer a blueprint for the way forward outside of dominant market interests. Their testimonies, like the one above, remind us that Black women are not only persistently confronting the twenty-first-century neoliberal hand they have been dealt but are teaching, publishing, serving, and defiantly transforming higher education both within and beyond the current entanglements of their colleges and universities.

Rosalind Gill (2009) suggests that, as academics, it is important that we critically look in our own backyard with a broad understanding of the relation between economic and political shifts, and transformations in work. In addition to the participants in this study offering keen institutional and structural analysis of the status and practices of higher education in the early twenty-first century, this group has a deep understanding of how these shifts are impacting their ability to teach effectively and reach students who are facing further social inequities. Their analysis and their collective experiences also expose the dire need in the United States to refund public education, restore social safety nets, and restore workers' rights that have eroded under austerity. Together their circumstances serve as pressure points of encounter for those who are concerned with the current state of higher education and social institutions at large. The testimonies in the foregoing chapters have exposed what is in disrepair in higher education and what it means to work within a social institution under siege by austerity and privatization. They also articulated the daily forms of resistance and existence that provide hints for future possibilities of regaining and reclaiming higher education as a social good.

Charli's statement in this chapter's epigraph reflects her intertwined pedagogical goals and her political agenda. Her educational agenda is not dissimilar from that articulated in *Higher Education for American Democracy: A Report of the President's Commission on Higher Education* (1947), more commonly known as the Truman Report, commissioned by President Truman, that advocated for racial, ethnic, gender, and also economic equality. Like Charli's perspective on higher education, this document proposed a grander plan and purpose for higher education in the United States, stating that American accomplishments "stop far short of our purpose. The discrepancies between America's democratic creed and how Americans live are still many and serious, [and] our society is plagued with inequalities, even in so fundamental a right as education" (12, 13).

Charli's commitments and others presented in this book not only evoke the social dreams of the Truman Report but also the forms of resistance-based praxis of progressive education reformers and the steadfast commitment to education by their forebears, who were denied access to resources, to education, and to intellectual and creative pursuits for centuries. To borrow Wanda Evans-Brewer's concept, they are indeed "jumping mountains" and in many ways steering us in the direction of education as a site to enact social justice and create a democratic society.

Their testimonies reveal that they are often deeply committed to the marginalized communities, subpopulations, and social issues with which colleges and universities purport to be aligned. They are coexisting at the intersection of a neoliberalizing university culture and a crumbling public sector. They are the recipients and stabilizers of the US efforts to economically, politically, and socially undermine the communities they are most concerned with. Their work also consistently defines the university's work as being connected to the welfare of the broader public sphere. In totality, their testimonies name the mass reform or interventions that need to take place both in and outside the university and offer compelling insights on how vast that impact could be if actualized on a grander scale. These efforts are encompassed in their expansive academic work. They advance models of pedagogical and intellectual resistance and offer resilient and subversive blueprints of a future university, one that must be reclaimed outside of market interests by imbuing its teaching, learning, innovation, and creativity, with a democratizing intention.

Their testimonies also suggest that reclaiming the university requires challenging the hegemony of intellectual traditions and policies that fail to capture the depth of the human condition and that limits our collective ability to respond to inequity and injustice. Their narratives remind us, as Mary Ellen Campbell and A. L. McCready have pointed out, that "there has never been such a dire need for decisive, anti-capitalist, anti-racist, anti-imperialist, anti-colonial, transnational feminist analysis, pedagogy and social foment" (2014, 1) in response to the university's current formation and practices. As such, their analytic reflections have collectively exposed the interconnections and necessary interventions between higher education, welfare reform, labor reform, and family policy in the United States.

Black Women's Critiques of Contemporary Higher Education

During a colloquium at Amherst College in 1980, Audre Lorde prophetically noted that the "institutionalized rejection of difference is an absolute necessity in a profit economy, which needs outsiders as surplus people." Her comments reflect a critical analysis of the mechanics of capitalism and operationalizes the political economies that undergird colleges and universities in the neoliberal era. Like Lorde, many Black academic feminists and other women of color feminists have been engaged in critique and theory making from within higher education long before the emergence of the subfield of critical university studies. Many bring histories of social uplift and visions of social justice with them as their catalyst for change in their quest for knowledge and access to higher education. Their writing has been vast on the subject of how to transform institutions of higher education, and many spend their working lives committed to transformational agendas in their classrooms, research, and leadership.

It is important to situate contemporary Black academic women's critiques of higher education even while knowing that "neoliberalism is coming for everyone." By doing so, I seek to highlight the differential impact neoliberal and corporate practices have on subgroups that are experiencing compounded forms of inequity. The women interviewed for this book organically extend the praxis of Black women academics who have come before them, but their analysis offers us an illustration of their racialized and gendered position within this massive economic onslaught on the current academic workforce. Interestingly, the majority of them willingly offered, often without prompting, critical analyses of the corporatized and privatized university and their vulnerability within these structures.

For instance, they each spoke freely about the broad range of academic labor practices, like retention services, that they were engaged in that were steeped in a climate that devalued them as racialized, gendered, and economically precarious academic workers. Niyah's assessment of her unacknowledged labor to retain students through mentorship not only exposed her understanding of the nuances of her exploitation as both a structurally and contractually contingent laborer, but it also demonstrated her understanding of how the larger social, political, and economic forces impacting her students' lives threaten their retention—and by association—her work as an educator and a graduate student. Niyah poignantly framed the socioeconomic landscape of the city she works in as a contributing factor to the personal and academic challenges her students faced:

> *The other part of that is I don't get paid for advising time. Memphis is a low-income city. It is a majority African American city. So, there are a lot of young, Black, single moms that end up in my class, and they want to come sit in my office and talk: "I really need to take a class but I don't have day care"; "My kids' dad is trippin'"—and I'm sitting here problem solving with them. I'm mentoring them and not having the proper mentorship myself. So, there's no compensation for all that.*

Additionally, Charli expressed her deep understanding of her institution's prioritization of research, a common trend across higher education settings beyond research universities as they jockey for position in rankings, a key factor in marketing their worth to prospective students. She described her own internal conflict as she weighs the significance of the increased demand and importance of research in relation to the imperative of educating as a praxis of democracy. She stated:

> *I am working through that. I feel that yes, we should do research projects because we need to train our students not only to be good scholars but also to do critical thinking. But I'm also very keen on being a good teacher as well, and not letting the research be the sole driver of your career. Students today in this time of standardized testing... they have limited critical thinking skills. They need reading teachers at the collegiate level! I think we need to reorient ourselves toward teaching, more rigorous teaching. A lot of people say, "Oh that's watering down the curriculum." No, it's not! It's the delivery style, not watering down the curriculum. If anything, we need to beef that curriculum up!*

Almost 60 years after the Truman Report, faculty like Charli celebrate the fruits of their labor when the futures of their students are at the center of their educational practice:

> *I get excited about these young people and teaching them and seeing them blossom. I like research, but I also love to teach my research. I don't like to do a bunch of research for the sake of what I call "linguistic acrobatics," so that I can impress my colleagues. Whenever I do research, I actually go back and teach it to my classes. And I love seeing my students blossom. They call me. They check in on Facebook. They said to me, "Hey, I went to grad school." I love hearing that because a lot of students I have taught, they couldn't even imagine going to college. Or maybe they were first generation. I love being that mentor for them. I love seeing them say, "Hey, I'm not going to let my environment or my past define me." I love being there for them now.*

Some may read her deep commitment in terms of her racialized and gendered position within higher education; however, there are other interpretations that can be helpful. One is that faculty, even exploited and undervalued faculty, have agency. They own their rationale for why and how they are engaging in the work. Charli's statement moves the actor beyond her own circumstances and demonstrates her unwavering commitment to advancing the purpose of higher education—as an intervention for those who are navigating inequality in society.

Still others openly acknowledge the benefits of the inclusive and accessible academic environment in community colleges, which is also under attack owing to massive federal defunding. These are the spaces where they reach much of the American public seeking a college education. This is especially true for people of color, parents, women, veterans, people with disabilities, first-generation students, and increasingly middle-class students. Charli explained the virtue of this work:

The environment itself was not a problem. I'll even say for the record—I enjoy teaching at the community college. I was able to teach people of all races, socioeconomic classes, learning abilities, and ages. In my classes, some of my students were older than I was. I enjoyed that because I thought it was very rewarding. I saw the difference that my teaching was making in my students' lives and how they were able to go on. Many of my students have gone on to get graduate degrees or better jobs. I see them around town.

She continued by suggesting that a return to an emphasis on teaching is imperative if we are to prepare our students to be critically engaged in global society. She also asserted that a renewed effort must be made to engage students who have been pushed to the margins within society and that she has faith in their ability to navigate beyond their circumstances if given the opportunity and if they are believed in. Charli represents the kind of committed educator that most colleges say they seek in their job descriptions and in their stated mission and marketing materials. Her enthusiastic comments also reflect her understanding of which groups are impacted by this level of intervention and the promise embedded in such social investment:

I want to prepare my students to meet a global challenge. "You are now citizens of the world"—that's the philosophy that I'm working through right now. I don't care where my students come from, I don't care what color they are, and I don't care about their socioeconomic status. I need you to look past your block and your family and your neighborhood and become critically thinking, global citizens of this world in this century. I feel that the educational model we have, the public school system and also at the collegiate level, which is so research-driven, I feel like it's not meeting those needs. I do. We are going to be servicing those kinds of students. Students from over in the South, a lot of black students come from Chicago, from Detroit, they come from Richland, California. These are students that no one has given a chance. This school where I'm working, they have a history of taking these students, and we can put them up against any student in America, any student who comes from a normal institution, they can write just as well when they finish. They can think and perform just as well. So I'm excited about that! Give them a chance and you'll be amazed at what people . . . People will surprise you.

Charli's critiques are aligned with those of other scholars who have been interrogating the role and function of the modern university. For instance, Christopher Newfield has argued that "public institutions cannot function properly as capitalist institutions. Their work of labor-intensive, craft-based creation and teaching is noncapitalist. Since capitalism will continue to insist on bottom-line measures of their output, universities will at those times need to be frankly anti-capitalist" (2011, 273). Newfield's position has been debated by others, but many of the testimonies in this book offer glimpses of hope that resist the capitalist intentions of academic institutions.

Still, identified threats to student learning are widespread, such as the massive diversion of institutional funds to skill-based and professionalized education, which have become increasingly prioritized over the goal to educate students to simply become the critically informed and engaged world citizens that Charli aims to produce. This false dichotomy that downplays the significance of critical thinking as part of any viable competency-based or professional training risks confusing and misleading students and their often indebted and anxious parents. Yet, David Shumway (2017) notes that "because neoliberalism rejects the very idea of 'not-for-profit' and insists that all values must be measured by the market, the humanities appear valueless. This has been a problem both for humanities enrollments and for the status of humanities disciplines within the university." The fallout has direct implications for women of color, including Black women, who are far more represented in the liberal arts than in STEM fields.

We most readily see evidence of this trend in the defunding, and in many cases, shuttering of many liberal arts and humanities academic programs, departments, and curricular requirements. Interestingly, this trend is coupled with an increased pressure for faculty across disciplines, beyond STEM, to document their worth by engaging in grant procurement that is increasingly entrepreneurial, can compromise academic integrity, and is ultimately of financial benefit to their university. In fact, in Molly McCluskey's (2017) recent report in the *Atlantic*, she noted that every university official she spoke with admitted that "corporate engagement in research is critical if universities are to continue their cutting-edge work" and that "university administrators not corporations were encouraging their faculty to be engaged in unregulated industry research that often is not the intellectual property of the faculty member or of benefit to their tenure and promotion portfolio." Even with these compromises, Shumway contends that "the competition for research contracts and philanthropic support was driven not only by a lack of public funding, but also the desire for higher status. Doubtless neoliberalism and the environment it fostered intensified this competition, but it did not bring it into existence."

Nonetheless, in order for faculty to be productivity driven and self-interested, often in order to secure their jobs, they turn inward and begin seeing teaching, particularly at the undergraduate level, as a project of managing bodies in order to generate more funds for colleges and universities. There is less institutional commitment to retention of US-born people of color, working-class and poor people, first-generation students, parents, and other groups that face mounting barriers to accessing higher education. A recent report from the Center on Budget and Policy Priorities (Mitchell et al. 2018) noted the average spending by states is 18 percent (or $1,598) less per student at public two- and four-year colleges and universities than before the Great Recession. This continued disengagement from the importance of and commitment to teaching has a wide, sweeping, and negative impact on students and was of concern for the faculty I interviewed. Even as the US economy has recovered after the 2008 recession, state and federal funding of higher education continues to be dismantled, threatening both teaching and learning (McCluskey 2017).

In a related vein, Annisha weighed in on the role of teachers and their potential impact on student learning and retention. She aligns the university's corporatized practices of faculty compensation with destabilizing the academic workforce:

> *They just didn't want to pay me. Instead of hiring me with the PhD, which they would have been obligated to pay more, they hired two [of] last year's degree people. They didn't even interview me. I have a history. You can look at my enrollment books and see that I have contributed to your student retention. Some students stayed here rather than go somewhere else to take my classes. They had their group of instructors that they liked. If you're really concerned about student retention wouldn't you want to keep the teachers around who contributed to your student retention?*

The twin crises of declining importance of teaching at many institutions and the increased casualization of academic labor are indicative of neoliberal practices, which shift public (in this case institutional) resources away from people and toward the institution's profits and corporate investments. Christopher Newfield's (2011) groundbreaking research outlines this shift by examining the case of New York University, which, in order to attract and hire renowned scholars, hired non-tenure-track faculty to teach their classes. These decisions have race, class, and gendered dimensions that are often not named in that most academic superstars are not faculty of color and even when they are, their representational expression of diversity does little to shift the exclusionary culture and practices of universities. These "bait and switch" transitions also do not ensure that students, particularly students of color, will gain access to the academic stars of color, who are often highly sought after and/or are overcommitted. Because adjuncts, like Annisha, are disproportionately women and academic stars are disproportionately male and white, her assessment of how she was faring in the hiring process is predictable. She is certain that her teaching has an impact and contributes to retention, but she also clearly understands that this appears not to be her university's highest priority. Though Annisha is an academic star in her own right, her talents as a retention-focused educator and her contributions to equity and justice within college settings are smothered in the restructured academic labor environment where contingent hires are increasing across institutions regardless of their rankings and the presence of superstars.

Finally, Marquita noted that she is fully aware of not only the systems that are exploiting her labor but also of the discourses surrounding that exploitation. She expressed a sense of ambivalence in that she fully understands what is at stake and why she should care about the academic labor movement, but she is also just trying to survive and make an income. She shared how she must balance the development of her intellectual aptitude within the context of demands of an educational system designed to exploit her labor:

But if you're an adjunct, you have to make decisions about where you want to plant yourself in that discourse. It's just that financially, that doesn't work. So, what do I want to do that is going to keep me engaged intellectually so I don't feel like I'm losing what I've been practicing as a teacher, but then get paid more than I would get paid as a teacher. How am I going to use all these skills in a way that benefits me, as opposed to all this stuff that I'm giving other people, and you're not really doing well in terms of how you are able to support yourself?

Here Marquita voices what many battleworn people of color allude to in labor struggles, but she also knows that as a primary breadwinner she and her family will benefit from the outcomes of an academic labor movement. She makes it clear that at some point she will have to make a forced choice in order to sustain herself financially. Eileen Schell has long critiqued the retrograde construction of academic women who work as adjuncts as simply satisfying their desire for "psychic income." This theorized form of gendered income that is characterized as a way to simply reward women for being engaged outside of the domestic sphere and engaged in a greater cause negates their work to stabilize their families and their demands to receive the wages they deserve. I call this state of being "ambivalence with clarity." Marquita also captured the shared sentiment of several of the academic women I interviewed regarding the tension between their desire to teach and conduct research at the postsecondary level and their demand for better pay and job security. They offered a clear analysis of their situation, noting that they are indeed breadwinners but also autonomous subjects who do not fall into the heteropatriarchal category of a kept and restless stay-at-home wife. Both their ambivalence and clarity are defining characteristics of their existence in higher education in this historical moment.

Resisting the Neoliberal and Corporatized University

Equally important to their analysis of the forces at play in contemporary US higher education institutions are a multitude of methods and approaches the participants in the current study used to subvert the market forces that were being imposed upon their education, their academic careers, and the organization of their private lives. Sara Motta contends that there is a need for us to assess "the revolutionary potentials of everyday forms of informal politics . . . which have historically been marginalised from the lens of masculinised revolutionary analysis" (2012, 3). The participants' cogent understanding of race, gender, and class inequities in society prepared and potentially emboldened them to identify and resist the imposition and intensification of these structures within a wide variety of contemporary academic settings.

One of the most compelling findings within the current study involved the participants' insistence on reframing the impact of such practices. They were all highly educated Black women, yet their experiences of structural and institutionalized racism and sexism were often articulated as forms of resistance and aligned with the broader struggles of other Black women. For instance, despite their trepidation—and at times, their articulations of internalized shame—they understood that securing financial support and resources from the state was critical, not only for their own and their family's economic survival but to ensure that they completed their graduate programs and/or continued pursuing the careers that they had sacrificed so much for. Black feminist economist Rhonda Williams, in her review of Black women economists' reflections on women and work, suggested, "In this ongoing era of white racial backlash, neither African Americans' access to higher education nor the benefits thereof are guaranteed"

(2002, 98). The participants' refusal to allow their dream of working as academics to be derailed, despite the onslaught of structural and institutionalized barriers they faced, demands that the world recognize their intellectual contributions and resists any subjugated position within an established, stratified, labor hierarchy.

In addition, as highly educated but precariously situated Black women, they reported being aware of and associated with the struggles of poor and working-class women. For instance, Stacey Patton's 2012 exposé, "The PhD Now Comes with Food Stamps," features an impoverished, white female adjunct professor whose very first statement denies that her economic circumstances should in any way be associated with the racially gendered trope of the "welfare queen." In contrast, the participants in the present study expressed what could be articulated as forms of political solidarity and often articulated the necessity for an intersectional understanding of and alignment with the gendered, race- and class-based struggles of Black women outside the university. They resisted what Yolanda Covington Ward (2013) defines as the "specter of the controlling image of the welfare queen," while also empathizing and often supporting other Black women facing economic inequity. For example, Brianna, a graduate student in social work who was receiving public assistance during her graduate studies, discussed the irony of her vulnerable economic standing as a graduate student and the importance of responding to the shared inequities she and her social work clients are navigating:

> I don't think that I get past the paradox of being educated, and yet facing some of the same challenges that our clients face. But we all need assistance to go wherever it is we're trying to go. I can't really separate myself or make myself seem like I'm better. What it has done

for me is it's allowed me to be more empathetic when working with my clients because I'm going through or I've been through some of the same things. And not to say that you have to go through it in order to [be] empathetic, because I don't think that's necessarily true. But I do feel like I really understand some of the stresses that they're facing and why their lives are so difficult, or sometimes they don't understand how to deal with some of the things that they're going through. And so if I can get through, it's my job and my duty to come back and help someone else to get through some of the same things that I was going through.

Here, Brianna not only empathizes with the women who will be her future clients, but she also frames the way in which higher education institutions have produced a destabilized and economically strained reality for her, and by association, others like her. The ballooning cost of graduate education has increasingly required intervention from the state to help graduate students survive, in many cases, for the first time in their lives. While the figures should not be overstated, it is notable that there is a documented rise in graduate students requiring public assistance and even a higher percentage of those who qualify but do not seek aid because of middle-class aspirational shame. What Brianna exposes is the failure of now-privatized universities that are producing her indebtedness, simply for seeking a graduate education and a career beyond the confines of working-class jobs and poverty wages.

Graduate students like Brianna are not alone. In fact, the number of adjunct faculty members, many of whom are also graduate students and now receive some form of public assistance, has skyrocketed. Recent data from the UC Berkeley Center for Labor Research and Education (Jacobs, Perry, & MacGillvary 2015) suggest that nearly a fourth of adjunct faculty are receiving some form of public benefits. In addition, they found that one in five families of part-time faculty receive earned income tax credit payments, and close to 100,000 part-time faculty members' families are enrolled in public assistance programs. Brianna's act of resistance via cross-class solidarity and her calling into question the political economies that produce these sorts of contradictions refer to what Sara Motta (2012) categorizes as contributing "to theories in solidarity within contemporary forms of anti-capitalist struggle."

While some participants have aligned themselves politically with the struggles of other Black women facing economic inequity, others have used their relative positions of power within higher education to confront the further consumption of Black women's literal and figurative bodies by refusing to engage in anything that demeans Black women's existence. As a dissenter, Drena underscores both her commitment to, and ownership of, a body of intellectual work with Black women as subjects, in spite of a context that has historically viewed their bodies as objects. She described during our interview how her intellectual work on eroticism as a way of life engaged Black women as sex workers but also disclosed that she noticed her research topic was of heightened interest to her white male dissertation committee. Despite her own vulnerable position as a structurally contingent academic subject, she reported that she pushed back against the patriarchal, racialized, and capitalist structure deeply embedded in the fabric of academic culture by refusing to allow her committee members to control or exploit the direction and content of her dissertation. She resurrected her protective defiance of that moment and stated, "I would not exploit Black women for their titillation." Drena's fierce protection of Black women's bodies asserted both her power over her intellectual process but also her decision to not deem her work as an economic transaction. In other words, she refused to sell her committee, composed largely of white men, the historically exploited and objectified body of Black women for her own professional gain—nor their consumption. Her protective actions are reminiscent of Ann duCille's (1994) early critique of the academy in which she proclaims that "the principal sites of exploitation are not simply the cabaret, the speakeasy, the music video, the glamour magazine; they are also the academy, the publishing industry, the intellectual community." Here duCille and Drena are affirming the literal and figurative bodies of Black women.

Drena unearthed additional layers of the systemic barriers facing Black women as structurally contingent academics by noting the constrained intellectual geography through which the academy often re-routes and controls them. She shared that when she was in the job market for a faculty position, the home department of her primary discipline was less interested in her scholarly contributions to her field and felt that she would best "fit" in minoritized fields like women's studies or Black studies. She respectfully refused such misdirected relocations, arguing that "I embrace the power of those critiques and lens but I have to earn my place in those departments." She interpreted her refusal to being intellectually boxed in, even in the midst of the hiring process, as an act of resistance. She reported that the attempts to steer her toward Black and women's studies programs emanated both from within her home department's refusal to value her entrance into that particular field but also from other structurally contingent and marginalized faculty members who were located within Black studies and who felt she should align with them politically in identity-based academic units regardless of her disparate scholarly focus. The pressure to align with identity-based units can be attributed to the enduring precariousness of these units within many academic institutions. Yet there is compelling evidence that intensified workloads and differing criteria for success exacerbate the vulnerability of faculty of color who hold joint appointments between a traditional department and an ethnic studies program or department (Cox 2008). For instance, the early but still compelling research of Robert Menges and William Exum found that faculty of color, like Drena, are often hired not only because of their identity of difference but also because they are presumed to have expertise in the fields of minority difference such as women's studies and ethnic studies. They then are hired with a joint appointment, often to their professional disadvantage. "The individual faculty member must manage 'two masters' and two sets of expectations" (1983/2016, 395). At first glance, this destabilizing practice may appear far from the brand of vulnerability than that of faculty who are navigating contractual vulnerability, but as I have argued earlier, these arrangements have historically placed minoritized faculty within academic units that are also underfunded and precariously situated, and thus their vulnerability is structurally produced as an often-unmarked form of contingency and disposability. Drena's analysis of her coerced intellectual displacement and her resistance to being hired under such conditions speaks to her demand to be recognized within the field she was trained to work within and on her own terms. Finally, in a joint blow of personal and professional self-preservation, Drena noted that she also refused to participate in what she observed as the unnecessarily intensified work culture of the current corporatized rendition of higher education, despite her intellectual promise and preparedness. Drena ultimately reported that she chose not to follow the traditional tenure-track route and said she did so in order to reject what she named as an extremely individualist, product-driven, and all-encompassing work culture that she felt devalued her as an intellectual, a woman, a person of color, and as a person with the desire to live an embodied life as a mother in the future.

Most participants reported an awareness of the means by which knowledge seeking and knowledge production have become commodified and the ways academic labor has become intensified and boundless under a corporatized labor model. While the dominant narrative about academic women—particularly underrepresented women of color—being "pushed out" is still empirically relevant, some participants in this study conveyed a counterpoint: they are active agents in their own lives and therefore were leaving on their own terms. They demanded that these decisions be understood as assertions of their power and individual agency. These contentions should not surprise readers of Black feminist theorists, particularly the work of Patricia Hill Collins, which has well documented the fact that Black women often reject the idea of being "passive victims [or] willing accomplices to their own oppression" (1989, 747).

For instance, when asked what led to her decision to leave higher education after years of hard work, Drena asserted:

> It's empowering to be able to make that decision on your own terms! Saying you have to leave. Matter of fact, the chair of my department has been in talks with other chairs and has written recommendations for me. For a while I was applying for positions in higher ed, faculty positions. The idea that the chair of my department, who is well-published, has said, "You have the ability to make your mark as a Black woman in this discipline, and you need not sell yourself short." That's empowering, to say that although these people have a certain belief in you, but you are willing to walk away and do something else. You believe that your capabilities do not stop here and that you have something of value to contribute to the rest of the world. That's empowering!

Charli articulated her personal agency, which is a critical building block in resisting systems of oppression and exploitation. Wanda Evans-Brewer also actively resisted being exploited as an adjunct laborer:

And what I put up is that this is not a story of victimization; it's a story of victory. I don't want anybody walking away seeing anything different. Because, at the end of the day, whether you make a million, whatever, you have to walk away with your soul. You have to make a decision early on. You choose between your hide and your soul. I choose my soul.

Wanda's declaration resonates with duCille and other Black feminists regarding Black women's agency as a site of resistance. DuCille's criticisms of academia largely reference the way Black women's bodies, pain, and labor are often co-opted for others' progress both inside and outside of academia. She criticizes Black women being othered and appropriated within both research agendas and political agendas and notes how their images are brandished to bolster others' interests and gains. Wanda articulated that she was maintaining her integrity when she asserted that she would not be manipulated, and that only she has control over her image, since she has been identified as a lightning rod within the contemporary academic labor movement. She adamantly declared, "All I can do is continue to be Wanda—Dr. Wanda J. Evans-Brewer. Whoever wants a piece of that pie, I'm willing to share it as long it don't humiliate me, you understand? It's not going to take my integrity. I'm good. I'll come speak. I'll come teach." Her clarity is notable, and she maintains a commitment to naming the forces at play, whether speaking on the contingent academic labor movement, the student loan debt crisis, or the realities of navigating poverty with a PhD. Here Wanda activates her agency as a site for resistance, both as an activist in the contingent labor movement and also as a Black woman cognizant of others' attempted manipulation of her labor and gendered and racialized image within such a movement.

Others resisted in the classroom, even when it was with some degree of uncertainty. The contemporary insistence, influenced heavily by the dominant research university model, that faculty members should maintain a social distance from their students, impacted the participants in this study. Even as Marquita tried to adopt this "keep them at arm's length" engagement strategy, she knew that the students who are most vulnerable require support beyond the stated curriculum. Her ambivalence about the dominant culture of disembodiment and disconnection from students' lives beyond the university was apparent. She confessed:

> I try not to get really attached to my students, and when I first started out, I had this assumption that you're not really supposed to interact with them at all outside of teaching, grading, and conferencing. But then you discover pretty quickly that there's an attachment embedded in essays, because I always start with the narrative essay, and they reveal very private things about themselves like without fail every semester, and so you immediately attach to them, you identify them with that narrative. You develop immediate concern when you read something. I don't really address it outside of the essay, though. I'm like "this is what you did structurally in this essay, and this is how we can improve it." And then, I'll ask them about themselves sometimes. You know, like "How've you been?" or "How's this going?" or whatever, but I try not to get too involved.

Marquita's internal struggle to maintain what has come to be labeled as "professional boundaries" is also informed by dominant models of engaging in market-driven, transactional intellectual work that is often disengaged from humanity and solidarity across life experiences. This subtle but effective cultural norm is predominant in research-focused academic settings and is believed to increase research-focused professors' productivity and protect their time. However, Marquita noted the sensitive ways in which she offers support in spite of the disembodied creep of the research-oriented, academic cultural norms:

Sometimes if they're not in class a lot, especially at this school and at my other community college, they'll tell you a really involved story. You know, like they had to go to court for child support. I'm just like, "I'm really sorry that you're going through these struggles," or "Let me know what I can do to support you." Actually, I did get asked that once to write a letter. This guy was a special case. He had been in the military, and he left it. He needed benefits because he had two kids, and he was trying to write this appeal letter. So he wasn't in class very much. When he would come to class he would show me all his military papers and stuff and [ask] can I help him write this six-page statement. And I did help, and I also gave him a letter. I was just like, "He wrote well and he was young, and he had a lot of struggles." If I could help at all with this then I will, 'cuz you know, but it's ... I don't know. It's hard for me to be like—I just don't want to get too attached. I had a girl this year—I usually have at least one pregnant mom—so there was a pregnant mom, and her baby was due before the semester was over. She had that baby and she e-mailed me. She was like, "I wasn't in class Friday because I had the baby." She came back to class on Monday. I was like, "Are you serious?" I said, "Well how's the baby?" She was like, "Fine!" I was like, "Okay." Yeah, so I don't know, I kind of do it case by case. They have a lot that they could tell you.

Marquita's response speaks not only to her connection to her students that exist outside of her time "on the clock" but also to the wide range of real-world student issues that committed adjunct faculty members are responding to in an attempt to retain their students. Despite problems ranging from child custody, to military commitments, to parenting, students are persisting, in part because adjunct faculty members are committed to their students' success—and to a degree that far exceeds their salaries, employment permanence, or other forces of destabilization at play within higher education. Some have argued, myself included, that these forms of committed labor are gendered and racialized and reflect forms of "institutional housekeeping" (Bird, Litt, & Wang 2004), "maternalized labor" (Nzinga-Johnson 2013), or those aspects of labor that are assigned to the "academic maids" (Harley 2008). These racialized and gendered descriptors attempt to capture the segmented and stratified placements of Black women and other women of color within the labor structure of higher education institutions (Acker 2006; Aguirre 2000; Trower & Chait 2002; Turner 2000, 2002; Turner & Myers 2000). Yet, the current study's participants' reframing of these forms of labor as acts of resistance against institutionally imposed boundaries acknowledges their deployment of personal agency. Their articulations of the labor practices they engaged in outside of capitalist intentions are notable and produce a viable model for those of us who struggle with demarcating where the outer boundaries of capitalism lie and where our anticapitalist humanity begins. It remains a challenge, however, to determine how to prevent such acts of rebellion from being exploited or marketed by self-interested academic institutions and to assure that faculty have agency and autonomy in deciding their level of desired engagement with students.

Additionally, persistence—whether that means staying enrolled in a PhD program or holding on to an academic career, even as an adjunct—is often evaluated as an indicator either of success or of poor decision making. I counter by suggesting that persistence can also be conceptualized as a form of resistance. When I asked Niyah, after several hours of her sharing a very traumatic graduate school experience, what her future plans were, she declared, "My goal is to teach in a women's studies program. I love women's studies. Of course, my degree is in sociology of gender with a focus on race and gender. That's my goal." Possessing clarity of purpose and aspiration despite the barriers she faces are forms of resistance that we often dismiss as masochism. Yet this is the degree of tenacity we hope for in those who are pursuing higher education and intellectual work. Moreover, Niyah's scholarly focus is within the interdisciplinary field of women's studies, despite its own institutional vulnerability. Our commitments to Black academic women, then, must include preserving the institutional spaces where they are likely to produce their work, namely, the interdisciplines.

Similarly, the participants in this study discussed their practices of decolonizing the curriculum and producing new forms of knowledge in higher education. They have fought to reimagine a social institution that engages a fuller array of thinkers and doers as guideposts for an envisioned intellectual tradition that is not controlled by an elite and powerful few but that represents the people of the society they seek to support. These are long-fought battles that have persisted as non-normative women have entered the academy.

Trice discussed her valiant attempts:

Quite frankly, the first year while I was on the ——— Fellowship, I thought to myself, "My check comes from somebody else and it comes from somebody who is specifically trying to infuse certain things into the curriculum. So when I come to you as my boss and it's like, "I'm going to teach this class called 'Women in blah, blah,' or 'Black

women in blah, blah,' I really don't want too much stuff from you."
So a constant battle about my classes, which was what I was brought
there to do.

She pointed out both her frustrations and her bewilderment about the need to engage in additional intellectual, political, and emotional work to reason with her colleagues about why their curriculum needed further development:

Then I get to the honors college and I try to get them to change some things in the curriculum. "Don't let me teach a class that's just African American or Black blah, blah. Let's do some things in the core curriculum that would introduce this to other places." At first, there were no African American readings. There's an honor seminar, like interdisciplinary that covers the great works of Western civilization and other pieces. I thought, "There's nothing by Black people, so we need to find some Black people. Can we get something in here by Black people?" [They replied], "You're making us tired." So I tried to introduce Toni Morrison. I tried to introduce Howard Thurman. I tried whatever. Every time I tried to introduce something else, I had to choose a reading. Then it had to go through the dog and pony show: "Now we're going to do a presentation where you present to all of us what the justification for this is." And you've said no anyway.

The sheer frustration is felt far and wide by faculty of color and other progressive faculty who are exasperated by the promises made in the diversity marketing strategies that are used to attract people of color to universities and are then withdrawn when they express unwillingness to forgo power.

Conclusion

These collectivist subjectivities fueled by histories of persistence and resistance coexist in the midst of what Mary Ellen Campbell and A. L. McCready suggest is "a rapidly accelerating culture of neoliberal individualism" (2014, 1). The Black women academics I interviewed found their futures and the futures of their students and their fellow colleagues more vulnerable than ever. Despite their compounded precarity, they continued to engage in the performance of care work on campus and remain committed to developing their intellectual work. These often racialized, gendered, and what I have called "maternalized" labor practices are messy, boundless, expected, and imposed. Despite the fact that these forms of labor are demanded from women of color faculty and function as invisible, uncompensated retention services with profit potential for self-serving institutions, the participants in the current project engaged in these practices beyond the self-interests of their institutions or the current marketized climate of higher education. Their analysis and acts of resistance aid us in creating a map of the way forward even at this vulnerable moment for many in higher education.

Conclusion

Statement of Solidarity

This book project ends where it did not begin. I initially conceptualized the conclusion as the final section of a manuscript in which I would encapsulate the key arguments of the previous chapters and offer some summary remarks about where I believed the state of US higher education was in this historical moment. I planned also to honor for one final time, the varied voices and rich analyses offered by the Black women academics whom I interviewed for the book. But I am no longer where I was—professionally, intellectually, nor politically—when I began this work. In many ways, I have moved on, but I still owe this book to them, the brave ones who dared to tell their truths. This conclusion is penned and this manuscript is finally complete with that sole commitment in mind. My primary objective has been to push through my own trepidations, be they structural or personal, and amplify their stories and brilliance.

I still plan to do so, but first humor me while I open this conclusion unconventionally, situating myself by integrating my social and political location within the larger framework and analysis of this project. I do realize that methodologically, conceptually, and theoretically it is a risk, but I need to be a bit disruptive in this moment. So I am choosing to present "additional data" in the conclusion. I am also suggesting and accepting, post hoc, that I am/was a "participant observer" in this project. I am being undisciplined by dabbling into autobiography, auto-ethnography, and even creative nonfiction as I close this project. I am breaking the rules in order to finish the book in a manner that feels authentic to me as an embedded woman of color feminist scholar of critical university studies. If I had not made this critical pivot in strategy, I may not have ever made it here.

Some may be curious to know how I came to almost abandon this critical body of work. For starters, I am no longer a tenure-track faculty member writing a single-authored book in order to gain tenure for the second time in my academic career. In fact, I am no longer a faculty member at all. To be fully transparent, I have changed jobs twice since I began writing this book. I left my prior academic institution in 2016 midway through my second tenure process to take a senior post with a health equity policy and research institute in Chicago. I was there for just over a year when I decided to return to higher education in 2017 but this time in an administrative role as the director of a campus-based women's center at an elite private university.

This new professional position means I also am no longer wed to the academic enterprise of prioritizing publishing over all other academic pursuits. In fact, I have never been committed to that brand of academic life. I have always revered my undergraduate professors who taught and were politically committed to the world beyond the university. They valued teaching and viewed it as a way to activate us as their students to become the citizens our world needs. They were my professional and political models, but somehow I digressed. My early years as a professor at a small liberal arts college were aligned with these values, but I soon learned that working at such institutions was looked down upon by those in more research-oriented academic settings. Somehow, I internalized valuing and becoming a "respected scholar" at an R1 research institution (doctoral university with very high research activity) and was re-socialized to distance myself from my students and my beloved craft of teaching in order to put my head down and "just write." I chose to write about Black women's precarious position within higher education in the new economy—an important project—but my productivity was driven by an R1 publish or perish tenure process. (In fact, during my new faculty orientation, even the dean of liberal arts and sciences at my former institution had instructed me to "focus on my writing and not so much on teaching.") This was the direct message to the faculty, despite the fact that the institution, which is located in Chicago, has an alarming rate of attrition among Black and first-generation students.

You may also be curious to know why someone who already had tenure would accept a position that required her to go through the process again, with even greater expectations for productivity. I, like many others who are part of dual career couples, found myself living and working in a city that I did not choose at the start of my academic career. I made the best of it and enjoyed the small liberal arts setting that valued teaching and service. I worked hard, and within seven years I had helped to found a master's of social work program and grew a women's studies minor into a major. I earned tenure and was promoted to the rank of associate professor because my institution valued my contributions in teaching, service, leadership, and scholarly engagement. However, neither I nor my partner wanted to remain in that part of the country, which had little opportunity for our three Black children. I personally had always wanted to teach at a historically Black college and university (HBCU) because I felt the students would appreciate me more as a professor, and I felt committed to affirming their intellectual curiosities and capacities in ways my former HBCU professors had done for me as a student. But after a decade of trying to coordinate job searches and gain dual offers, we finally found ourselves with an opportunity to move to a larger, vibrant, and more diverse city and to an R1 institution. The one caveat was that my partner was the lead candidate and had just published a book, so he was recruited and hired with tenure at the associate rank. I, on the other hand, was offered a tenure-track position but would be required to go through the tenure process for the second time.

As further water-under-the-bridge context, I birthed two of my children during my PhD program and one as an early junior faculty member. I was not granted parental leave in either instance but was somehow supposed to be as "productive" as my peers. Of course I did finish my PhD program, and I was successful as a professor in the liberal arts context, but I did not have what more resourced academics would call a robust research agenda, publication record, or academic footprint to hold on to my hard-earned senior position. And if I were honest, I would also say that I, too, at some point must have begun to devalue my prior accomplishments and internalized the academy's hierarchical messaging about what forms of academic work "count" and "matter." So I accepted the tenure-track position with reduced pay but with research support and went from an associate professor of social work and director of women's and gender studies to an assistant professor of gender and women's studies.

Words cannot express the pain of having a decade of one's intellectual and professional work erased. I was grateful to have been offered a tenure-track position as a "trailing" spouse, but walking into my office each day with the title of "assistant professor" attached to my door was soul zapping. Still I taught, I served on committees, I published, I expanded my professional network, I connected with my wonderful new students and colleagues, and I tried to hold the weight of my very heavy heart and head high.

After four years of agreeing to re-earn my title as a tenured and associate professor, I boldly decided that I had enough of proving myself to a system that I felt refused to see and appreciate my worth and my well-established career as a college professor. Deciding that I deserved to be valued and remembering my own merit, I left behind the academic career I had been building since 1995. That also meant I left with this book half written and with an accompanying severely wounded ego. Somehow, I had become a character in my own story—a Black academic woman pushed out (chapter 4).

Some might argue that I left on my own will and that I had choice and agency at every turn. I agree that I did and do have individual agency, but choice is a liberal conceptualization that fails to take into account one's full access to institutions. Arguing we all have "choice" is a form of misguided victim blaming. When we leave our hard-earned, beloved careers and institutions there are always structural forces at play. Some seem obvious—race- and gender-based injustice and inequity. Other forms, especially those that are contemporarily at play, like neoliberal orientations toward work, can be harder to see. Even I did not fully see what was often operating around me and the insidiousness in which I may have been complicit. Rosalind Gill reminds us, "Neoliberalism found fertile ground in academics whose predispositions to 'work hard' and 'do well' meshed perfectly with its demand for autonomous, self-motivating, responsibilised subjects" (2009, 248).

But now I have taken a giant step back, and my lens, tongue, and spine have sharpened. Nineteen years after graduating with my PhD, I still have ballooning six-figure student loan debt, so my brain is, essentially, "mortgaged" (chapter 1). While I am one of the lucky ones who landed a tenure-track position right out of graduate school, I was hired at a salary rate that could never pay off my loans. I also am a Black, first-generation college graduate from a working-class family, with no family wealth, so my student loans were much higher because I needed them for my undergraduate and graduate studies and living expenses. My partner and I also inherited each other's educational debts when we were forced to consolidate them early in our academic careers. Unfortunately, he inherited a greater amount of debt from me, because he grew up middle class, completed his undergraduate studies at an in-state university, and benefited from financial support from his family. After 15 years of paying our student loans, they have only ballooned. Now that I have two children in college, I have been forced to take out even more student loans as a result of not being able to save for their college education because we had to pay for child care for three children, repay my and partner's student loans, and pay high taxes and a mortgage in order to live in a suburban public school district that might give our racially marked children a fighting chance. I am not sure where retirement will take me with the incredible burden of educational debt that I currently carry for four of my family members.

I am grateful to have never experienced the vulnerability of being *contractually* contingent, but I have always been *structurally* contingent and disposable as a first-generation, college-educated Black woman and mother. I was the first Black woman at my former institution to gain tenure in 21 years. I belong to the 2 percent of Black women in the United States who earn PhDs and an even smaller number who gain tenure and the rank of full professor. I labored as a professor but was structurally punished for still not being the right type of academic when I needed to move to another institution. My institutional commitments—from academic program building to teaching to mentoring to student retention—were structurally made invisible. My first book, which was published within the first year of my second tenure process, was institutionally diminished because it was collaborative and not single-authored. This approach to knowledge production and scholarship was intentional and was aligned with my political and professional values as a woman of color feminist scholar, but my first book was ultimately "weighted" as a journal article, which my research-oriented, rankings-conscious institution felt was not even worthy of negotiating higher pay or tenure at my point of hire. My decade of work was not transferable or translatable, even in the field of women's and gender studies. It had no value. It was erased. This is a structural vulnerability that Black women face whether they are tenure-track or not and whether or not they are in academic units that have political histories of resistance against dominant ways of producing knowledge and ascertaining success. We are often committed to innovation in the classroom and in our scholarship. We are often engaged in community work. These contributions are seized upon by the university's marketing teams, but they are used against us to justify our dismissal or, in my case, demotion and ousting (chapter 2).

As I mentioned previously, I gave birth to my children in graduate school and as a junior professor, without any institutional support. No time off was granted in either position. Conversely, public assistance representatives offered varying forms of hostile and dehumanizing material support. I had no choice but to use my student loans to pay for food, housing, and child care to survive and stay on course with my career. Even with a gainfully employed cisgender, heterosexual male partner who also has a tenure-track position, I could not afford to pay my (nor his) student loans and day care when I began my career, so I had to ask for forbearances for almost five years, until my youngest child began kindergarten. Neither of our early career institutions offered on-campus child care or child care subsidies, so we could only afford day care for two to three days a week. We were often home with our children on days we did not teach, which impacted our ability to be more engaged in our careers and campus life. In many ways, we were like migrant workers who are isolated from extended family networks and supports.

My partner's early career fared slightly better because his former institution offered junior sabbaticals, but he did not receive parental leave when our daughter was born. I was granted the semester off when she was born but had to negotiate that arrangement by agreeing to front-load my fall teaching load in the summer prior to her birth. I felt appreciative of the accommodation, given that my institution did not have a maternity leave policy for faculty, but one of my senior white male departmental colleagues asserted that I should only be excused from my teaching duties, not my administrative duties, which required me to negotiate another level of accommodation with the chairperson of my department. This was in the department of social work, so navigating institutionalized sexism in an intellectual space that is organized around advocating for people's social needs was especially challenging and disappointing. I was also expected to write a journal article in order to justify not teaching in the fall semester during which I had my daughter. I completed and submitted the article before I returned to campus in the spring, but it was rejected during the journal review process. Given that I was nursing a newborn and caring for two other children while also functioning on very little sleep, I am comfortable stating that my submission, written under those conditions, was simultaneously subpar and extraordinary (chapter 3).

For the past four years, I have tried to keep my distance from the bloody guts of this book, but I now realize that I have been standing at the scene of the crime this whole time. With time away to simply sit in this heaviness of a semi-complete project, I was finally able to see the connective and entangled threads between my own experiences in higher education, those of my study's participants, and the larger phenomenon that is hyperproducing inequity for so many Black academic women.

I have been the invisible "character" or "patient zero" throughout this whole academic endeavor, and am now able to fully acknowledge why this book has been so painful to write and complete. I drafted the introduction and the first three chapters prior to leaving my faculty post at my former R1 academic institution. I attempted to draft chapter 4 while working my nine-to-five post-academic policy job. But every time I picked it up, I felt nothing but dread and avoided the project, because my own wounds were so fresh. Somehow in the course of writing this book, unbeknown to me, I had become one of the many former Black academic women who are now on the outside looking in and wondering what went wrong with our professional trajectories. I finally drafted "Jumping Mountains" almost two years after leaving my hard-earned career as a professor. Penning that final chapter required me to emotionally numb myself to get words on the page. In addition, this conclusion has been waiting in the wings owing to yet another job transition in the past three years. Changing jobs abruptly is highly unusual for me. I spent 11 years gaining a substantial education that prepared me for an academic career and had been employed as a faculty member since earning my doctorate. But in 2012, I found myself destabilized by a major cross-country move with a family of five and transitioning between three jobs in six years. I strug-

gled through multiple job transitions and managing the associated anxiety and mood-related symptoms to get to this
point. The coincidental ache of this book—one that exposes
and maps the neoliberal impact on Black academic women's
lives, including my own—has been a heavy cross to bear.

I know that I have already thanked my editorial team in the
acknowledgments, but I must thank them again here. Jeffery
Williams and Greg Britton held space for me through this
hard-fought intellectual and psychic crisis. I also thank Julia
Jordan Zachary, Michelle Boyd, Nadine Naber, and Kim
Greenwell, who all represent women of color who understood my pains on a deep spiritual level and who reminded
me of who I was and why our stories need to be seen in the
light. I continue to be undisciplined by naming these individuals here, because part of the academic enterprise is to follow
the rules and erase labor. We have labored collectively, and
this book and the Critical University Studies series are about
recognizing academic labor, so honoring these individuals
here is fitting to me as both author and their comrade. The
publication of this book has become less about the publish or
perish terror of the tenure process for me. It has become a
space for me to offer my analysis of what I bore witness to as a
marginalized academic since the fall semester of 1995 when I
naively began my doctoral studies and believed that academic
institutions embodied their stated values. I became a participant observer, and this book encapsulates the complexity of
my phenomenological observations as a displaced Black academic woman. I have learned from the women who shared
their stories that they hold the answers to our collective
futures in higher education.

Black women and other underrepresented women of
color academics continue to serve as a critical starting point
from which to confront the massive loss and exploitation of

intellectual workers in the academy. In them we find the invisible body, the sexualized body, the gendered body, the racialized body, the underpaid body, the unpaid body, the contingent body, the teaching body, the uninsured body, the pregnant body, the caregiving body, and we find the servant body of both community and academic institutions. All these pressure points demand our attention and intervention if we are to steer the university on course toward justice. This work is complex and enduring, but the late Toni Morrison (2015) offered a grounding thought as she reflected on the state of the world: "I know the world is bruised and bleeding, and though it is important not to ignore its pain, it is also critical to refuse to succumb to its malevolence. Like failure, chaos contains information that can lead to knowledge—even wisdom." The current neoliberal chaos in higher education also contains our collective wisdom to produce the answers for a way forward. The university, "with all its limitations remains a location of possibility. In that field of possibility we have the opportunity to labor for freedom, to demand of ourselves and our comrades, an openness of mind and heart that allows us to face reality even as we collectively imagine ways to move beyond boundaries, to transgress. This is education as the practice of freedom" (hooks 1994).

The women who shared their personal and professional lives with me were aware of the mountains they faced but moved through the world with transformative perspectives about higher education and viewed education as the practice of freedom. In turn, we must demand comprehensive responses from higher education institutions because they have not been passive victims, but instead have been active agents, in the exploitation of their workers and students. The United States has $1.5 trillion in student loan debt that continues to balloon well past consumer debt, affecting millions of Americans—and Black women and their families disproportionately. The academic labor movement is mobilizing across the world but continues to be tone deaf to the persistence and complexity of race and gender labor disparities here in the United States. Universities still do not provide adequate paid family leave, child care support, elder care, and other worker entitlements that caregiving faculty, staff, and students require to be successful. The Trump administration continues to rapidly dismantle the nation's already vulnerable public safety net and social institutions en masse. Though classes begin like clockwork each fall, colleges and universities are in free-falling crisis as they move away from the idea of education as a public project and adopt at full scale the notion that it is a product to be marketed, sold, and purchased.

This book serves as a call to action by amplifying the voices of promising and prophetic Black academic women and by mapping the impact of the current inhumane and market-driven practices of higher education on their lives. Their collective testimonies demand that we place value on their intellectual labor and humanity and offer us a counterexample against the dominant narratives on diversity and inclusion. It is time that we reclaim political ownership of our country's social institutions in order to stabilize the hemorrhaging of Black academic women students and faculty. If we truly listen to them, both as theorists and as testifiers, then we may be able to redress the most critical threats to higher education in this historical moment.

Appendix A

Our Truths Interview Guide

First Interview

Part One: Introduction

1. Review purpose of study and protocol, and gain consent signature
2. Choose pseudonym

Part Two: Interview Guide

Self-Reported Demographic Information
Age:
Race/ethnicity:
Highest level of education:
Gender:

General Questions

1. Why did you go to graduate school?
2. What does gaining a college education mean to you?
3. What does the term "educational justice" mean to you?
4. Do you believe there are any barriers that Black women face if they are interested in graduate education?
5. Do you personally face any of those barriers?
6. What are you most proud of concerning your graduate school journey?
7. What fears do/did you have about being on this journey?
8. Were you able to be hired as a professor following graduate school? If so, are you tenure-track or non-tenure-track?

Family Responsibilities: Tell me more about your family
responsibilities

1. Do you have any dependents at home?
2. Number of:
3. _____ children (0–6 yrs.); _____ (7–14 yrs.); _____ (15+ yrs.)
4. _____ family members with disabilities
5. _____ elderly
6. Are you the primary breadwinner for your household?
7. Do you have health insurance?
8. Do you have reliable child care / elder care?

Community Involvement: Tell me more about your community
engagement

1. Are you involved in any initiatives outside of your school work? If
   yes, which ones?
2. How many hours do you spend per month on community-based
   initiatives?
3. What are your motivations for working on these initiatives?
4. Do you feel there are any connections between your university
   work and your community work? If so, in what ways?

Economic Status: Tell me about your economic status

1. What is your current annual income (under 20K annually;
   21K–40K, 41K–60K; 61K–80K; 81K–100K; more than 100K)?
2. Does your income cover all of your living expenses? If not, are
   there other ways in which you supplement your income?
3. Do you supplement your income with public assistance? With
   other forms of private support (family, friends, etc.)?
4. Since you have been a graduate student: Have you or your family
   ever gone hungry? Had utilities shut off? Been evicted? Had your
   car repossessed? Been without health insurance?

Graduate School Experience

1. Did you receive funding from your graduate program?
2. How has your financial investment in graduate school impacted
   your financial status currently or upon graduation?

3. What level of student loans do you currently have?
4. Does your level of educational debt impact your decisions about your professional or educational future? In what ways?

Faculty Experience

1. What is your current position/title?
2. How long have you worked as an adjunct professor?
3. How many courses do you teach per semester? How many students are enrolled? Do you have a teaching assistant?
4. How many hours per week do you spend teaching (in class, grading, preparation, etc.)?
5. How would you describe the nature of your involvement with your students?
6. What is the focus of your doctoral work?
7. How much time do you spend writing or working on your dissertation per week?
8. Are there other non-academic jobs where you also work? Hours per week?
9. How would you describe your teaching/work schedule?

Health Status: Tell me about your overall health

1. How would you describe your overall health status? What factors do you think contribute to your health?
2. Do you have both formal and informal support systems? If so, how do they specifically support you as a student/professor? As a caregiver?
3. How would you describe your stress level? What factors contribute to your stress? Which factors buffer it?
4. How would you describe your overall mental health status? What factors do you think contribute to your health—positively and negatively?

Second Interview

After coding and analysis of the first interview, a second interview will be scheduled if needed. This interview will include follow-up questions that emerged from the preliminary data analysis in the first interview. Prior to this interview, the co-researcher/participant will have already received a transcription of the first interview. The second interview will begin with a discussion about whether the first interview adequately described what the co-researcher/participant wanted to share about the topics.

Potential Probes

- Could you tell me more about . . . ?
- Is there anything else I should know that I didn't ask that would be helpful to this project?
- Could you share some examples of your experience as a part-time/ non-tenure-track professor and/or a parent/caregiving graduate student / faculty member?
- Are there topics that you feel are important that need to be explored and/or explored in more depth by this study?

Resources and Organizations

Academic Associations and Professional Supports

American Association of Blacks in Higher Education (AABHE)
American Association of University Women (AAUW)
Association of Black Women in Higher Education (ABWHE)
Association of Higher Education Parent / Family Program
    Professionals (AHEPPP)
Caucus on Academic and Community Activism of the American
    Studies Association
Committee on Contingent Labor in the Profession, Modern
    Language Association (MLA)
Contingent Faculty Interest Group of the National Women's
    Studies Association (NWSA)
Feminist Campus Faculty and Staff Network of the New Feminist
    Majority
National Postdoctoral Association
National Women's Studies Association (NWSA)
New Feminist Majority
Women in Higher Education (WIHE)
Working Class Studies Association

Academic Labor Resources

(Compiled by Kira Schuman, Midwest Lead Organizer, American
Association of University Professors)
    American Association of University Professors (AAUP)
    American Federation of Labor and Congress of Industrial
        Organizations (AFL-CIO)

American Federation of Teachers (AFT)

Canadian Association of University Teachers (CAUT)

Coalition of Contingent Academic Labor (COCAL)

Coalition of Graduate Employee Unions (CGEU)

National Education Association (NEA)

New Faculty Majority (NFM) Service Employees International Union (SEIU)

Unemployment Compensation for Contingent Faculty, AAUP

United Auto Workers (UAW)

United Electrical, Radio and Machine Workers of America (UE)

Academic-Life Resources

Beneath the Façade

Brilliance Remastered

Campus Pride Index

Creating a Family Friendly Department: Chairs & Deans Toolkit by UC Family Friendly Edge

InkWell Academic Writing Retreats

Pregnant Scholar

Public Service Loan Forgiveness Program

University of California, Hastings College of Law, WorkLife Law
  Effective Union Representation of Pregnant and Parenting Employees Faculty
  Gender Bias Learning Project
  Retention and Advancement of Faculty
  WorkLife Law Attorney Network

Advocacy Organizations

American Council on Education (ACE)

Campaign for the Future of Higher Education

College and University Professional Association for Human Resources (CUPA-HR)

Consumer Financial Protection Bureau[1]

Federal Trade Commission

Human Rights Campaign

Institute for College Access and Success

Institute for Women's Policy Research
National Association of Consumer Advocates
National Women's Law Center National Student Legal Defense
    Network
Student Debt Crisis
Transgender Law Center

Practical Supports

Children's Health Insurance Program (CHIP)
Housing: Subsidized housing, housing vouchers, public housing,
    and Low Income Home Energy Assistance Program (LIHEAP)
Medicaid
Medicare
Supplemental Nutrition Assistance Program (SNAP)
Supplemental Security Income (SSI)
Temporary Assistance for Needy Families (TANF)
Therapy for Black Girls
Unemployment Insurance

Relevant US Federal Legislation

Affordable Care Act (ACA) of 2010
Americans with Disabilities Act (ADA) of 1990
Civil Rights Act of 1964
Consumer Credit Protections Act of 1968
Equal Employment Opportunity Act of 1972
Fair Credit Billing Act of 1974
Fair Debt Collection Practices Act (FDCPA) of 1977
Family and Medical Leave Act (FMLA) of 1993
Institutional Accountability regulations of 2019
Pregnancy Discrimination Act of 1978
Title IX of the 1972 Educational Amendments of the 1964 Civil
    Rights Act
Title VII of the Civil Rights Act of 1964
Truth in Lending Act of 1968
Unemployment Insurance, Social Security Act of 1935
Violence against Women Act of 1994

Notes

Introduction
Epigraph: Vanessa Marr, "Teaching for Change: Notes from a Queer Black Hustling Mama," in *Laboring Positions: Black Women, Mothering and the Academy*, ed. Sekile Nzinga-Johnson (Toronto: Demeter Press), 60.

1. Black academic women and other women of color scholars have been active and persistent interrogators of the exclusionary culture and exploitative practices of the university though their theorizations but are often erased from the genealogy of studies critical of the university. See the writings of Lorde (1984), James and Farmer (1993), duCille (1994), hooks (1994), Benjamin (1997), Turner (2002), Cox (2008), Harley (2008), Collins (2013), and McMillan Cottom (2017) for a cursory review of their antiracist, anticapitalist, academic labor, and feminist contributions that inform the academic subfield of critical university studies.

2. Feminists and critical university scholars whose work centers on the casualization and feminization of the academic workforce and the corporatization and privatization of higher education have also informed the current study. See Adair and Dahlberg (2003), Pratt (2004), Acker (2006), Bousquet (2008, 2012), Massé and Hogan (2010), and Williams (2013, 2014) for a further reading.

3. See Fernández Arrigoitia et al. (2016) for a discussion of the importance of these identity- and employment-based protections.

Chapter 1. Mortgaging Our Brains
Epigraph: Charli, interview with author.

1. Steven Pitts, "Research Brief: Black Workers and the Public Sector," UC Berkeley Labor Center, http://laborcenter.berkeley.edu/pdf/2011/blacks_public_sector11.pdf.

2. See "The Personal Responsibility and Work Opportunity Reconciliation Act of 1996," US Department of Health and Human Services, Office of the Assistant Secretary for Planning and Evaluation, https://aspe.hhs.gov/report/personal-responsibility-and-work-opportunity-reconciliation-act-1996.

3. See "Tale of Two Recoveries: Economic Recoveries of Black and White Homeowners," American Civil Liberties Union (ACLU), https://www.aclu .org/report/tale-two-recoveries-economic-recoveries-black-and-white -homeowners.

4. Matthew Desmond, "Poor Black Women Are Evicted at Alarming Rates," MacArthur Foundation, http://www.macfound.org/media/files /HHM_Research_Brief_-_Poor_Black_Women_Are_Evicted_at_Alarm ing_Rates.pdf.

5. For a historical review of Black women's economic position in the United States, see Jones (1985), Amott & Matthaei (1996), White (1999), and Mutari, Power, & Figart (2002).

6. See Survey of Earned Doctorates, table 19, "Doctorate Recipients, by Ethnicity, Race, and Citizenship Status: 2003–13," http://www.nsf.gov /statistics/sed/2013/data/tab19.pdf.

7. See "The Student Debt Cliff," Student Labor Action Project, http:// studentlabor.org/2013/05/17/the-student-debt-cliff.

8. View and/or read the "Remarks by the President," http://www .bloomberg.com/news/articles/2015-01-21/full-transcript-of-obama-s-2015 -state-of-the-union-address.

9. For examples of the corporatization of higher education that took place during the Obama administration, see "Wall Street: The Real University President," Student Labor Action Project, http://studentlabor.org/action.

10. Graduate education is a "growth industry" in the United States. The number of master's degrees conferred per year has more than tripled from nearly 236,000 in 1970 to about 759,000 in 2015 (US Department of Education). For further discussion of the current economies of graduate education in the United States, see *PBS NewsHour*, https://www.pbs.org /newshour/education/graduate-programs-become-cash-cow-struggling -colleges-mean-students.

11. See discussion of "Cohort Default Rates" at Institute for College Access and Success, https://ticas.org/our-work/accountability/cohort-default-rates.

12. Extreme debt has been defined as educational debt exceeding $20,000.

13. See "How America's Student Debt Crisis Impacts Black Students," Business Insider, https://www.businessinsider.com/how-americas-student-debt -crisis-impacts-black-students-2019-7; and "African Americans, Student Debt and Financial Security," Demos, http://demos.org/sites/default/files/publications /African%20Americans%20and%20Student%20Debt%5B7%5D.pdf.

14. See Survey of Earned Doctorates, table 19, "Doctorate Recipients, by Ethnicity, Race, and Citizenship Status: 2003–13," http://www.nsf.gov /statistics/sed/2013/data/tab19.pdf.

15. For a general discussion of exploitive labor conditions cloaked in the rhetoric of "love," see "Why 'Do What You Love' Is Pernicious Advice,"

Atlantic, https://www.theatlantic.com/business/archive/2015/08/do-what
-you-love-work-myth-culture/399599; and for feminist critiques of academic
labor, see "Institutional Feelings: Practicing Women's Studies in the Corporate University," *Feminist Formations*, https://www.feministformations.org
/blog/institutional-feelings-practicing-women%E2%80%99s-studies
-corporate-university-feminist-formations-273.

Chapter 2. Ain't I Precarious?

Epigraph: Wanda Evans-Brewer, interview with author.

1. Marni [pseudonym], "Adjuncts Should Do as Little Work as Possible,"
Adjunct Project blog, September 29, 2013, accessed February 23, 2015,
http://adjunct.chronicle.com/adjuncts-should-do-as-little-work-as-possible.

2. The documentary *Con Job: Stories of Adjunct and Contingent Labor* can
be watched in its entirety via YouTube, https://www.youtube.com/watch?v
=SlmWBEz4bf0, or via the website of its distributor/publisher, Computers
and Composition Digital Press, http://ccdigitalpress.org/conjob.

3. See Maisto's post on *Working-Class Perspectives* (blog), https://
workingclassstudies.wordpress.com/2013/09/23/adjuncts-class-and-fear.
Note that Chad Roscoe's comments that were read when the article was
accessed on January 11, 2015, are now removed (https://workingclassstudies
.wordpress.com/2013/09/23/adjuncts-class-and-fear/#comments).

4. See, for other examples, Donato DeSimone, "Adjunct Professors:
America's Modern Slaves?," *Times Herald* columns, July 6, 2012, accessed
January 11, 2015, http://www.timesherald.com/article/JR/20120706
/OPINION03/120709706; and Lisa Benavides, "Slave Labor in Higher Ed?
The Adjuncts," H-Net: Humanities and Social Sciences Online discussion
page, February 28, 1995, accessed January 11, 2015, http://h-net.msu.edu/cgi
-bin/logbrowse.pl?trx=vx&list=h-teach&month=9502&week=e&msg
=c%2BbosycIsAnapu%2BqlxCV/Q&user=&pw.

5. Victoria Hay, "Adjunct Work as 'Slave Labor': A Fair Comparison?,"
Daily Adjunct blog, May 2, 2014, accessed January 11, 2015, http://adjunct
.chronicle.com/adjunct-work-as-slave-labor-a-fair-comparison.

6. Shonda Goward, cited in Joseph Fruscione, "Adjunct Pay and Anger,"
Adjuncts Interviewing Adjuncts column, *Inside Higher Ed*, August 27, 2014,
accessed February 23, 2015, https://www.insidehighered.com/advice/2014/08
/27/adjunct-interviews-adjunct-pay-and-working-conditions.

7. See Gwendolyn Beetham's full article, "Love in a Time of Contingency:
A Letter to Women's and Gender Studies," at Feminist Wire, https://
thefeministwire.com/2014/07/womens-and-gender-studies.

8. NWSA, "Contingent Faculty Solidarity Statement," February 9, 2016,
NWSA Statements, National Women's Studies Association, https://www
.nwsa.org/content.asp?pl=19&contentid=104#ContingentFaculty.

9. See "Women's Studies and Complicity: Between Exploitation and Resistance," LSE Research Online, https://core.ac.uk/download/pdf/35437251.pdf.

10. See "Institutional Feelings: Practicing Women's Studies in the Corporate University," *Feminist Formations* 27(3) (Winter 2015).

11. New Faculty Majority: Women in Contingency Project, accessed December 20, 2019, http://www.newfacultymajority.info/women-and-contingency-project.

Appendix B. Resources and Organizations

1. The Trump administration's secretary of education, Betsy DeVos, withdrew a series of the Obama administration's policy memos that aimed to protect student loan borrowers. Several states have now begun crafting their own legislation to protect consumers of student loans. In 2019, seven states passed laws requiring loan servicing agencies to adhere to consumer protection requirements.

Bibliography

Introduction

Acker, Joan. 2006. "Inequality Regimes: Gender, Class, and Race in Organizations." *Gender & Society* 20(4) (August): 441–64. doi:10.1177/0891243206289499.

Adair, Vivyan C., and Sandra Dahlberg, eds. 2003. *Reclaiming Class: Women, Poverty, and the Promises of Higher Education in America*. Philadelphia: Temple University Press.

American Federation of Teachers (AFT). 2011. *Promoting Gender Diversity in the Faculty: What Higher Education Unions Can Do*. Washington, DC: American Federation of Teachers. http://files.eric.ed.gov/fulltext/ED520168.pdf.

American Institutes for Research. 2013. "The Price of a Science PhD: Variations in Student Debt Levels across Disciplines and Race/Ethnicity." Broadening Participation in STEM Graduate Education. Issue brief. http://www.air.org/sites/default/files/downloads/report/AIRPriceofPhDMay13_0.pdf.

Benjamin, Lois. 1997. *Black Women in the Academy: Promises and Perils*. Gainesville: University Press of Florida.

Bousquet, Marc. 2008. *How the University Works: Higher Education and the Low-Wage Nation*. New York: New York University Press.

———. 2012. "Lady Academe and Labor-Market Segregation." *Chronicle of Higher Education* (October 29). http://chronicle.com/article/Lady-AcademeLabor-Market/135284.

Carr, Felicia. 2001. "The Gender Gap in the Academic Labor Crisis." *Minnesota Review* 52–54 (Fall): 271–79.

Castaneda, Mari, and Kirsten Isgro, eds. 2013. *Mothers in Academia*. New York: Columbia University Press.

Chang, Mariko. 2010. *Lifting as We Climb: Women of Color, Wealth and America's Future*. Oakland, CA: Insight Center for Community Economic Development. https://insightcced.org/old-site/uploads/CRWG/LiftingAsWeClimb-WomenWealth-Report-InsightCenter-Spring2010.pdf.

Collins, Patricia Hill. 1986. "Learning from the Outsider Within: The Sociological Significance of Black Feminist Thought." *Social Problems* 33(6): S14–S32.

———. 2013. *On Intellectual Activism*. Philadelphia: Temple University Press.

Cox, Aimee. 2008. *Women of Color Faculty at the University of Michigan: Recruitment, Retention, and Campus Climate*. Report prepared for the University of Michigan Center for the Education of Women. http://www.cew.umich.edu/wp-content/uploads/2018/06/AimeeCoxWOCFull2_3.pdf.

Curtis, John W., and Saranna Thornton (for the American Association of University Professors). 2014. *Losing Focus: The Annual Report on the Economic Status of the Profession*. http://www.aaup.org/file/zreport.pdf.

Dill, Bonnie Thornton, and Ruth Zambrana, eds. 2009. *Emerging Intersections: Race, Class, and Gender in Theory, Policy, and Practice*. New Brunswick, NJ: Rutgers University Press.

duCille, Ann. 1994. "The Occult of True Black Womanhood: Critical Demeanor and Black Feminist Studies." *Signs* 19(3): 591–629.

Ferguson, Roderick A. 2012. *The Reorder of Things: The University and Its Pedagogies of Minority Difference*. Minneapolis: University of Minnesota Press.

Fernández Arrigoitia, M., Gwendolyn Beetham, Cara E. Jones, and Sekile Nzinga-Johnson. 2016. "Women's Studies and Contingency: Between Exploitation and Resistance." *Feminist Formations* 27(3): 81–113. Project MUSE. https://muse.jhu.edu.

Giroux, Henry A., and Kostas Myrsiades, eds. 2013. *Beyond the Corporate University: Culture and Pedagogy in the New Millennium*. Lanham, MD: Rowman & Littlefield.

Gould, Elise, Zane Mokhiber, and Julia Wolfe. 2018. *Class of 2018*. Economic Policy Institute. https://www.epi.org/files/pdf/147514.pdf.

Gutiérrez y Muhs, Gabriella, Yolanda Flores Niemann, Carmen G. González, and Angela P. Harris, eds. 2012. *Presumed Incompetent: The Intersections of Race and Class for Women in Academia*. Boulder: University Press of Colorado. Published by Utah State University Press.

Harley, Debra A. 2008. "Maids of Academe: African-American Women Faculty at Predominately White Institutions." *Journal of African American Studies* 12: 19–36.

hooks, bell. 1990. "Homeplace." In *Yearning: Race, Gender, and Cultural Politics*. Boston: South End Press.

———. 1994. *Teaching to Transgress: Education as the Practice of Freedom*. New York: Routledge.

James, Joy, and Ruth Farmer, eds. 1993. *Spirit, Space, and Survival: African American Women in (White) Academe*. New York: Routledge.

Johnson, Anne, Tobin Van Ostern, and Abraham White. 2012. *The Student Debt Crisis*. Washington, DC: Center for American Progress. https://cdn .americanprogress.org/wp-content/uploads/2012/10/WhiteStudentDebt -5.pdf.

Lorde, Audre. 1984. *Sister Outsider: Essays and Speeches*. Trumansburg, NY: Crossing Press.

Marr, Vanessa. 2013. "Teaching for Change: Notes from a Broke Queer Hustling Mama." In *Laboring Positions: Black Women, Mothering and the Academy*, ed. Sekile Nzinga-Johnson, 58–71. Toronto: Demeter Press.

Massé, Michelle A., and Katie J. Hogan, eds. 2010. *Over Ten Million Served: Gendered Service in Language and Literature Workplaces*. Albany, NY: SUNY Press.

McMillan Cottom, Tressie. 2014a. "New Old Labor Crisis." *Slate*, January 24. http://www.slate.com/articles/life/counter_narrative/2014/01/adjunct _crisis_in_higher_ed_an_all_too_familiar_story_for_black_faculty.html.

———. 2014b. "Slavery Should Never Be a Metaphor." *Adjunct Project* (blog), May 5. http://adjunct.chronicle.com/slavery-should-never-be-a-metaphor.

———. 2017. *Lower Ed: The Troubling Rise of For-Profit Colleges in the New Economy*. New York: New Press.

Metzger, Jack. 2013. "We Are Worth More." Working Class Studies. https:// workingclassstudies.wordpress.com/2013/05/06/we-are-worth-more.

Mohanty, Chandra Talpade. 2013. "Transnational Feminist Crossings: On Neoliberalism and Radical Critique." *Signs* 38(4) (Summer): 967–91.

Mullings, Leith. 2000. "African-American Women Making Themselves: Notes on the Role of Black Feminist Research." *Souls* 2(4): 18–29. doi:10.1080/10999940009362233.

Newfield, Christopher. 2011. *Unmaking the Public University: The Forty-Year Assault on the Middle Class*. Cambridge, MA: Harvard University Press.

Nixon, Laura. 2013. "The Right to (Trans) Parent: A Reproductive Justice Approach to Reproductive Rights, Fertility, and Family-Building Issues Facing Transgender People." *William & Mary Journal of Women and the Law* 20(1): https://scholarship.law.wm.edu/wmjowl/vol20/iss1/5.

Nzinga-Johnson, Sekile, ed. 2013. *Laboring Positions: Black Women, Mothering and the Academy*. Toronto: Demeter Press.

Osei-Kofi, Nana. 2012. "Junior Faculty of Color in the Corporate University: Implications of Neoliberalism and Neoconservatism on Research, Teaching, and Service." *Critical Studies in Education* 53(2) (June): 229–44.

Pratt, Minnie Bruce. 2004. "Taking the Horizon Path: Keynote at the NWSA in New Orleans, LA, on June 19, 2003." *NWSA Journal* 16(2) (Summer): 15–33.

Ross, Andrew. 2012. "Anti-Social Debts." *Contexts* 11(4) (November 16): 28–32. http://journals.sagepub.com/doi/pdf/10.1177/1536504212466328.

Schell, Eileen E. 1998. *Gypsy Academics and Mother-Teachers: Gender, Contingent Labor, and Writing Instruction*. Portsmouth, NH: Boynton.

Temple, Brandie. 2017. "Despite Job Growth, Black and Latina Women Are Still Being Left Behind." National Women's Law Center. https://nwlc.org /blog/despite-job-growth-black-and-latina-women-are-still-being-left -behind.

Turner, Caroline Sotello Viernes, and Samuel L. Myers. 2000. *Faculty of Color in Academe: Bittersweet Success*. Boston: Allyn and Bacon.

US Department of Education. 2011. *Employees in Postsecondary Institutions, Fall 2009, and Salaries of Full-Time Instructional Staff, 2009–10*. Washington, DC: National Center for Education Statistics. http://nces.ed.gov /pubs2011/2011150.pdf.

US House Committee on Education and the Workforce. 2014. *The Just-in-Time Professor: A Staff Report Summarizing eForum Responses on the Working Conditions of Contingent Faculty in Higher Education*. http:// democrats.edworkforce.house.gov/sites/democrats.edworkforce.house .gov/files/documents/1.24.14-AdjunctEforumReport.pdf.

Ward, Kelly, and Lisa Wolf-Wendel. 2012. *Academic Motherhood: How Faculty Manage Work and Family*. New Brunswick, NJ: Rutgers University Press.

Williams, Jeffrey. 2013. "The Great Stratification." *Chronicle of Higher Education* (December 2). http://chronicle.com/article/The-Great Stratification/143285.

———. 2014. "The Remediation of Higher Education and the Harm of Student Debt." *Comparative Literature* 66(1): 43–51.

Chapter 1. Mortgaging Our Brains

Adair, Vivyan, and Sandra Dahlberg. 2003. "Introduction: Reclaiming Class; Women, Poverty, and the Promise of Higher Education." In *Reclaiming Class: Women, Poverty, and the Promise of Higher Education in America*, ed. Vivyan Adair and Sandra Dahlberg, 1–20. Philadelphia: Temple University Press.

Amott, Teresa, and Julie Matthaei. 1996. *Race, Gender, and Work: A Multicultural Economic History of Women in the U.S.* Boston: South End Press.

Bair, C. R., and J. G. Haworth. 2006. "Doctoral Student Attrition and Persistence: A Meta-Synthesis of Research." In *Higher Education: Handbook of Theory and Research*, ed. J. C. Smart, 19: 481–534. Dordrecht: Kluwer Academic Publishers.

Bousquet, Marc. 2008. *How the University Works: Higher Education and the Low-Wage Nation*. New York: New York University Press.

Chang, Mariko. 2010. *Lifting as We Climb: Women of Color, Wealth, and America's Future*. Oakland, CA: Insight Center for Community Economic

Development. Accessed August 3, 2015. https://insightcced.org/old-site /uploads/CRWG/LiftingAsWeClimb-WomenWealth-Report-InsightCenter -Spring2010.pdf.

DiTomaso, Nancy. 2012. *The American Non-dilemma: Racial Inequality without Racism.* New York: Russell Sage Foundation.

Ellis, E. M. 2001. "The Impact of Race and Gender on Graduate School Socialization, Satisfaction with Doctoral Study, and Commitment to Degree Completion." *Western Journal of Black Studies* 25(1): 30–45.

Gutiérrez y Muhs, Gabriella, Yolanda Flores Niemann, Carmen G. González, and Angela P. Harris, eds. 2012. *Presumed Incompetent: The Intersections of Race and Class for Women in Academia.* Boulder: University Press of Colorado. Published by Utah State University Press.

Johnson, Anne, Tobin Van Ostern, and Abraham White. 2012. "The Student Debt Crisis." Center for American Progress. https://www.americanprogress .org/wp-content/uploads/2012/10/WhiteStudentDebt-3.pdf.

Jones, Jacqueline. 1985. *Labor of Love, Labor of Sorrow: Black Women, Work, and the Family from Slavery to the Present.* New York: Basic Books.

Maddix, Marcelle, and LaToya Sawyer. 2013. "I Am My Child's First Teacher: Black Motherhood and Homeschooling as Activism within and beyond the Academy." In *Laboring Positions: Black Women, Mothering, and the Academy*, ed. Sekile Nzinga-Johnson, 75–90. Toronto: Demeter Press.

Mutari, Ellen, Marilyn Power, and Deborah M. Figart. 2002. "Neither Mothers nor Breadwinners: African-American Women's Exclusion from US Minimum Wage Policies, 1912–1938." *Feminist Economics* 8(2): 37–61.

Neem, Johann N., Brenda Forster, Sheila Slaughter, Richard Vedder, Tressie McMillan Cottom, and Sara Goldrick-Rab. 2012. "The Problem with For-Profits in the Education Assembly Line." *Contexts* 11(4): 14–21.

Nzinga-Johnson, Sekile, ed. 2013. *Laboring Positions: Black Women, Mothering, and the Academy.* Toronto: Demeter Press.

Paisley, Jane Harris. 2003. "Gatekeeping and Remaking: The Politics of Respectability in African American Women's History and Black Feminism." *Journal of Women's History* 15(1): 212–20.

Patton, Stacey. 2012. "The PhD Now Comes with Food Stamps." *Chronicle of Higher Education* (May 6). Accessed August 3, 2015. http://chronicle.com /article/From-Graduate-School-to/131795.

Perlow, Olivia N., Sharon L. Bethea, and Durene I. Wheeler. 2014. "Dismantling the Master's House: Black Women Faculty Challenging White Privilege/Supremacy in the College Classroom." *Understanding and Dismantling Privilege* 4(2): 241–59.

Rogers, Juhanna Nicole. 2015. "On the Burdens Carried by Single Black Mothers Enrolled in PhD Programs." For Harriet, March 4. Accessed

August 3, 2015. http://www.forharriet.com/2015/03/the-burdens-carried
-by-single-black.html#axzz3eTAxxthS.

Turner, Caroline Sotello Viernes, and Samuel L. Myers. 2000. *Faculty of Color in Academe: Bittersweet Success*. Boston: Allyn and Bacon.

White, Deborah Gray. 1999. "Making a Way Out of No Way." Chapter 7 in *Too Heavy a Load: Black Women in Defense of Themselves, 1894–1994*. New York: W. W. Norton.

Williams, Jeffrey. 2014. "The Remediation of Higher Education and the Harm of Student Debt." *Comparative Literature* 66(1): 43–51.

Zeiser, Kristina L., Rita J. Kirshstein, and Courtney Tanenbaum. 2013. "The Price of a Science PhD: Variations of Student Debt Levels across Disciplines and Race/Ethnicity." Center for STEM Education and Innovation. http://www.air.org/sites/default/files/downloads/report /AIRPriceofPhDMay13_0.pdf.

Chapter 2. Ain't I Precarious?

Ahmed, Sara. 2012. *On Being Included: Racism and Institutional Life*. Durham, NC: Duke University Press.

American Federation of Teachers (AFT). 2010. *Promoting Racial Diversity in the Faculty: What Higher Education Unions Can Do*. Washington, DC: AFT Higher Education.

———. 2011. *Promoting Gender Diversity in the Faculty: What Higher Education Unions Can Do*. Washington, DC: AFT Higher Education.

Baldwin, Roger G., and Jay L. Chronister. 2001. *Teaching without Tenure: Policies and Practices for a New Era*. Baltimore, MD: Johns Hopkins University Press.

Beetham, Gwendolyn. 2014. "Love in the Time of Contingency: A Letter to Women's and Gender Studies." Feminist Wire. Accessed December 20, 2019. https://thefeministwire.com/2014/07/womens-and-gender-studies.

Benavides, Lisa. 1995. "Slave Labor in Higher Ed? The Adjuncts." H-Net: Humanities and Social Sciences Online discussion page, February 28. http://h-net.msu.edu/cgi-bin/logbrowse.pl?trx=vx&list=h-teach&month =9502&week=e&msg=c%2BbosycIsAnapu%2BqlxCV/Q&user=&pw.

Benjamin, Ernst. 2002. "How Over-Reliance on Contingent Appointments Diminishes Faculty Involvement in Student Learning." *AACU Peer Review* 5(1) (Fall): 4–10.

Benjamin, Lois. 1997. *Black Women in the Academy: Promises and Perils*. Gainesville: University Press of Florida.

Bousquet, Marc. 2008. *How the University Works: Higher Education and the Low-Wage Nation*. New York: New York University Press.

———. 2012. "Lady Academe and Labor-Market Segregation." *Chronicle of Higher Education*, October 29. http://chronicle.com/article/Lady -AcademeLabor-Market/135284.

Burgan, Mary. 2010. "Careers in Academe: Women in the 'Pre-Feminist' Generation in the Academy." In *Over Ten Million Served: Gendered Service in Language and Literature Workplaces*, ed. M. A. Massé and K. J. Hogan, 23–34. Albany, NY: SUNY Press.

Carr, Felicia. 2001. "The Gender Gap in the Academic Labor Crisis." *Minnesota Review* 52–54 (Fall): 271–79.

Chatterjee, Piya, and Sunaina Maira, eds. 2014. *The Imperial University: Academic Repression and Scholarly Dissent*. Minneapolis: University of Minnesota Press.

Coalition on the Academic Workforce (CAW). 2012. *A Portrait of Part-Time Faculty Members: A Summary of Findings on Part-Time Faculty Respondents to the Coalition on the Academic Workforce Survey of Contingent Faculty Members and Instructors*. http://www.academicworkforce.org/CAW _portrait_2012.pdf.

Cox, Aimee. 2008. *Women of Color Faculty at the University of Michigan: Recruitment, Retention, and Campus Climate*. Report prepared for the University of Michigan Center for the Education of Women. http://www.cew .umich.edu/wp-content/uploads/2018/06/AimeeCoxWOCFull2_3.pdf.

DeSimone, Donato. 2012. "Adjunct Professors: America's Modern Slaves?" *Times Herald*, July 6. http://www.timesherald.com/article/JR/20120706 /OPINION03/120709706.

De Welde, Kristine, and Andi Stepnick, eds. 2014. *Disrupting the Culture of Silence: Confronting Gender Inequality and Making Change in Higher Education*. Sterling, VA: Stylus.

Donoghue, Frank. 2008. *The Last Professors: The Corporate University and the Fate of the Humanities*. New York: Fordham University Press.

duCille, Ann. 1994. "The Occult of True Black Womanhood: Critical Demeanor and Black Feminist Studies." *Signs* 19(3): 591–629.

Ferguson, Roderick A. 2012. *The Reorder of Things: The University and Its Pedagogies of Minority Difference*. Minneapolis: University of Minnesota Press.

Fruscione, Joseph. 2014. "Adjunct Pay and Anger." Adjuncts Interviewing Adjuncts column, Inside Higher Ed website, August 27. https://www .insidehighered.com/advice/2014/08/27/adjunct-interviews-adjunct-pay -and-working-conditions.

Gappa, Judith M., and David W. Leslie. 1993. *The Invisible Faculty: Improving the Status of Part-Timers in Higher Education*. San Francisco: Jossey-Bass.

Graduate Student Employees Organization (GSEO, Yale University). 2005. *The (Un)Changing Face of the Ivy League*. New Haven, CT: GSEO.

Gutiérrez y Muhs, Gabriella, Yolanda Flores Niemann, Carmen G. González, and Angela P. Harris, eds. 2012. *Presumed Incompetent: The Intersections of Race and Class for Women in Academia*. Boulder: University Press of Colorado. Published by Utah State University Press.

Hanks, Lawrence J., Jas Sullivan, Sara B. Spencer, and Elgin Rogers. 2008. "Affirmative Action, the Academy and Compromised Standards: Does Affirmative Action Lower Standards in University Hiring, Tenure and Promotion?" *Forum on Public Policy: A Journal of the Oxford Round Table* (Summer 2008): http://forumonpublicpolicy.com/summer08papers /archivesummer08/hanks.pdf.

Harley, Debra. 2008. "Maids of Academe: African-American Women Faculty at Predominately White Institutions." *Journal of African American Studies* 12: 19–36.

Hay, Victoria. 2014. "Adjunct Work as 'Slave Labor': A Fair Comparison?" *Daily Adjunct* (blog), May 2. http://adjunct.chronicle.com/adjunct-work -as-slave-labor-a-fair-comparison.

James, Joy, and Ruth Farmer, eds. 1993. *Spirit, Space, and Survival: African American Women in (White) Academe*. New York: Routledge.

Karabel, Jerome. 2005. *The Chosen: The Hidden History of Admission and Exclusion at Harvard, Yale, and Princeton*. New York: Houghton Mifflin.

Leonard, David. 2013. "Adjuncts Aren't Slaves: Let's Stop Saying That They Are." *Chronicle Vitae* (blog), December 4. https://chroniclevitae.com /news/200adjunctsaren-t-slaves-let-s-stop-saying-they-are.

Maisto, Maria. 2013. "Adjuncts, Class, and Fear." *Working-Class Perspectives* (blog). September 23. http://workingclassstudies.wordpress.com/2013 /09/23/adjuncts-class-and-fear.

Marginson, Simon. 2006. "Dynamics of National and Global Competition in Higher Education." *Higher Education* 52: 1–39.

Marr, Vanessa. 2013. "Teaching for Change: Notes from a Broke Queer Hustling Mama." In *Laboring Positions: Black Women, Mothering and the Academy*, ed. Sekile Nzinga-Johnson, 58–71. Toronto: Demeter Press.

Massé, Michelle A., and Katie J. Hogan, eds. 2010. *Over Ten Million Served: Gendered Service in Language and Literature Workplaces*. Albany, NY: SUNY Press.

McMillan Cottom, Tressie. 2014a. "New Old Labor Crisis." *Slate*, January 24. http://www.slate.com/articles/life/counter_narrative/2014/01/adjunct _crisis_in_higher_ed_an_all_too_familiar_story_for_black_faculty .html.

———. 2014b. "Slavery Should Never Be a Metaphor." *Adjunct Project* (blog), May 5. http://adjunct.chronicle.com/slavery-should-never-be-a-metaphor.

Modern Language Association (MLA). 1994. "MLA Statement on the Use of Part-Time and Full-Time Adjunct Faculty Members." Modern Language Association, February. http://www.mla.org/statement_faculty.

Mohanty, Chandra Talpade. 2013. "Transnational Feminist Crossings: On Neoliberalism and Radical Critique." *Signs* 38(4) (Summer): 967–91.

National Women's Studies Association Contingent Faculty Interest Group. 2015. "Contingent Faculty Resolution #1." National Women's Studies Conference, San Juan, Puerto Rico.

Newfield, Christopher. 2011. *Unmaking the Public University: The Forty-Year Assault on the Middle Class*. Cambridge, MA: Harvard University Press.

Nzinga-Johnson, Sekile, ed. 2013. *Laboring Positions: Black Women, Mothering and the Academy*. Toronto: Demeter Press.

Olssen, Mark, and Michael A. Peters. 2005. "Neoliberalism, Higher Education and the Knowledge Economy: From the Free Market to Knowledge Capitalism." *Journal of Education Policy* 20(3): 313–45.

Osei-Kofi, Nana. 2012. "Junior Faculty of Color in the Corporate University: Implications of Neoliberalism and Neoconservatism on Research, Teaching, and Service." *Critical Studies in Education* 53(2) (June): 229–44.

Patitu, Carol Logan, and Kandace G. Hinton. 2003. "The Experiences of African American Women Faculty and Administrators in Higher Education: Has Anything Changed?" Special issue. *New Directions for Student Services* 104: 79–93.

Pratt, Minnie Bruce. 2004. "Taking the Horizon Path: Keynote at the NWSA in New Orleans, LA, on June 19, 2003." *NWSA Journal* 16(2) (Summer): 15–33.

Ross, Andrew. 2017. "The Mental Labor Problem." In *Class: The Anthology*, ed. Stanley Aronowitz and Michael J. Roberts, 1–31. Hoboken, NJ: John Wiley & Sons.

Schell, Eileen E. 1998. *Gypsy Academics and Mother-Teachers: Gender, Contingent Labor, and Writing Instruction*. Portsmouth, NH: Boynton.

Schreker, Ellen. 2010. *The Lost Soul of Higher Education: Corporatization, the Assault on Academic Freedom, and the End of the American University*. New York: New Press.

Schuster, Jack H., and Martin J. Finkelstein. 2006. *American Faculty: The Restructuring of Academic Work and Careers*. Baltimore, MD: Johns Hopkins University Press.

Slaughter, Sheila, and Gary Rhoades. 2009. *Academic Capitalism and the New Economy: Markets, State, and Higher Education*. Baltimore, MD: Johns Hopkins University Press.

Steffan, Heather. 2010. "Intellectual Proletarians in the Twentieth Century." *Chronicle of Higher Education*, November 28. http://chronicle.com/article /Intellectual-Proletarians/125477.

Turner, Caroline Sotello Viernes. 2002. "Women of Color in Academe: Living with Multiple Marginality." *Journal of Higher Education* 73(1): 74–93.

Turner, Caroline Sotello Viernes, and Samuel L. Myers. 2000. *Faculty of Color in Academe: Bittersweet Success*. Boston: Allyn and Bacon.

US Department of Education. 2011. *Employees in Postsecondary Institutions, Fall 2009, and Salaries of Full-Time Instructional Staff, 2009–10*. Washington, DC: National Center for Education Statistics. http://nces.ed.gov /pubs2011/2011150.pdf.

US House Committee on Education and the Workforce. 2014. *The Just-in-Time Professor: A Staff Report Summarizing eForum Responses on the Working Conditions of Contingent Faculty in Higher Education*. http:// democrats.edworkforce.house.gov/sites/democrats.edworkforce.house .gov/files/documents/1.24.14-AdjunctEforumReport.pdf.

Vargas, Lucila, ed. 2002. *Women Faculty of Color in the White Classroom*. New York: Peter Lang.

Waltman, Jean, and Carol Hollenshead. 2007. *Creating a Positive Departmental Climate: Principles for Best Practices*. Ann Arbor: University of Michigan Center for the Education of Women.

Williams, Jeffrey J. 2013. "The Great Stratification." *Chronicle of Higher Education*, December 2. http://chronicle.com/article/The-Great -Stratification/143285.

Xiaotao Ran, Florence, and Di Xu. 2018. "Does Contractual Form Matter? The Impact of Different Types of Non-Tenure Track Faculty on College Students' Academic Outcomes." *Journal of Human Resources* (May 4). doi: 10.3368/jhr.54.4.0117.8505R.

Chapter 3. Families Devalued

American Association of University Women (AAUW). 2004. *Tenure Denied*. Washington, DC: American Association of University Women Educational Foundation and the American Association of University Women Legal Advocacy Fund.

American Institutes for Research. 2013. "The Price of a Science PhD: Variations in Student Debt Levels across Disciplines and Race/Ethnicity." Broadening Participation in STEM Graduate Education. Issue brief. http://www.air.org/sites/default/files/downloads/report/AIRPriceofPhD May13_0.pdf.

Bracken, Susan, Jeanie Allen, and Diane Dean. 2006. *The Balancing Act: Gendered Perspectives in Faculty Roles and Work Lives*. Sterling, VA: Stylus.

Chan, Adrienne, and Donald Fisher. 2008. *Exchange University: Corporatization of Academic Culture*. Vancouver: University of British Columbia Press.

Collins, Patricia Hill. 1987. "The Meaning of Motherhood in Black Culture and Black Mother/Daughter Relationships." *SAGE Journal* 4(2): 7.
———. 1994. "Shifting the Center: Race, Class, and Feminist Theorizing about Motherhood." In *Mothering: Ideology, Experience, and Agency*, ed. Evelyn Nakano Glenn, Grace Chang, and Linda Forcey, 45–65. New York:

Routledge; and simultaneously in *Representations of Motherhood*, ed. Donna Bassin, Margaret Honey, and Meryle Kaplan, 56–74. New Haven, CT: Yale University Press.

Crosby, Faye J., Joan C. Williams, and Monica Biernat. 2004. "The Maternal Wall." *Journal of Social Issues* 60(4): 675–82.

Evans, Elrena, and Caroline Grant. 2008. *Mama PhD: Women Write about Motherhood and Academic Life*. New Brunswick, NJ: Rutgers University Press.

Frasch, Karie, Mary Ann Mason, Angy Stacy, Marc Goulden, and Carol Hoffman. 2007. *Creating a Family Friendly Department: Chairs and Deans Toolkit*. UC Faculty Friendly Edge. https://ucfamilyedge.berkeley.edu/sites/default/files/chairsanddeanstoolkitfinal7-07.pdf.

Gilens, Martin. 1999. *Why Americans Hate Welfare: Race, Media, and the Politics of Antipoverty Policy*. Chicago: University of Chicago Press.

Jacobs, Ken, Ian Perry, and Jenifer MacGillvary. 2015. *The High Public Cost of Low Wages: Poverty-Level Wages Cost U.S. Taxpayers $152.8 Billion Each Year in Public Support for Working Families*. Research brief. Berkeley, CA: UC Berkeley Center for Labor Research and Education.

Leonard, Pauline, and Danusia Malina. 1994. "Caught between Two Worlds: Mothers as Academics." In *Changing the Subject: Women in Higher Education*, ed. Sue Davies, Cathy Lubelska, and Jocey Quinn. Abingdon, UK: Taylor and Francis.

Mason, Mary Ann, Marc Goulden, and Nicholas Wolfinger. 2006. "Babies Matter: Pushing the Gender Equity Revolution Forward." In *The Balancing Act: Gendered Perspectives in Faculty Roles and Work Lives*, ed. Susan Bracken, Jeanie Allen, and Diane Dean. Sterling, VA: Stylus.

Motta, Sara. 2012. "The Messiness of Motherhood in the Marketised University." Beautiful Transgressions column, *Ceasefire* (June). http://ceasefiremagazine.co.uk/messiness-motherhood-marketised-university.

Neubeck, Kenneth, and Noel Casenave. 2001. *Welfare Racism: Playing the Race Card against America's Poor*. New York: Routledge.

Nielsen, Laura, Robert Nelson, and Ryon Lancaster. 2010. "Employment Discrimination Litigation in the Post Civil Rights United States." *Journal of Empirical Legal Studies* 7(2) (June): 175–201.

Noll, Elizabeth, Lindsey Reichlin, and Barbara Gault. 2017. *College Students with Children: National and Regional Profiles*. Washington, DC: Institute for Women's Policy Research. https://iwpr.org/wp-content/uploads/2017/02/C451-5.pdf.

O'Brien Hallstein, Lynn, and Andrea O'Reilly. 2012. *Academic Motherhood in a Post–Second Wave Context: Challenges, Strategies and Possibilities*. Toronto: Demeter.

Patton, Stacey. 2012. "The PhD Now Comes with Food Stamps." *Chronicle of Higher Education* (May 6). Accessed August 3, 2015. http://chronicle.com /article/From-Graduate-School-to/131795.

Pearson, A. Fiona. 2007. "The New Welfare Trap: Case Managers, College Education, and TANF Policy." *Gender & Society* 21(5) (October): 723–48. doi:10.1177/0891243207306381.

Stone, Pamela. 2007. *Opting Out? Why Women Really Quit Careers and Head Home*. Berkeley: University of California Press.

Sullivan, Beth, Carol Hollingshead, and Gilia Smith. 2004. "Developing and Implementing Work-Family Policies for Faculty Author(s)." *Academe* 90(6) (November–December): 24–27. Accessed August 30, 2013. http://www.jstor.org/stable/40252702.

Treisman, Rachel. 2019. "New SNAP Rule Impacts College Students by Limiting Benefits and Adding Confusion." NPR. https://www.npr.org /2019/12/21/789295697/new-snap-rule-impacts-college-students-by -limiting-benefits-and-adding-confusion?fbclid=IwARorsiErs _T3q6dRwnNRn4ca6ToYqfc1rowa_niZHFd0R5akBBHB6fpeeqk.

Ulrich, Laurel Thatcher. 1982. *Good Wives: Image and Reality in the Lives of Women in Northern New England, 1650–1750*. New York: Alfred A. Knopf.

US Department of Health and Human Services. Administration for Children and Families. 2006. "Reauthorization of the Temporary Assistance for Needy Families Interim Final Report." *Federal Register* 71(125) (June 29): 37453–83.

US Department of Labor. 2019. Employment and Training Administration. *Unemployment Insurance*. Accessed December 20, 2019. https://oui.doleta .gov/unemploy.

Williams, Joan. 2012. "Double Jeopardy? How Gender Bias Differs by Race." Presentation at the National Academies' conference "Seeking Solutions: Maximizing American Talent by Advancing Women of Color in Academia," June 7–8, Washington, DC.

Chapter 4. Jumping Mountains

Acker, Joan. 2006. "Inequality Regimes: Gender, Class, and Race in Organizations." *Gender & Society* 20(4) (August): 441–64. doi:10.1177/0891243206289499.

Aguirre, Adalberto, Jr. 2000. *Women and Minority Faculty in the Academic Workplace: Recruitment, Retention, and Academic Culture*. ASHE-ERIC Higher Education Report, vol. 27, no. 6. Jossey-Bass Higher and Adult Education Series. https://eric.ed.gov/?id=ED447752.

Bird, Sharon, Jacquelyn S. Litt, and Yong Wang. 2004. "Creating Status of Women Reports: Institutional Housekeeping as 'Women's Work.'" *NWSA Journal* 16(1): 194–206. Accessed September 1, 2019. https://muse.jhu.edu.

Campbell, Mary Ellen, and A. L. McCready. 2014. "Issue Introduction: Materialist Feminisms against Neoliberalism." *Politics and Culture* (March 9). https://politicsandculture.org/2014/03/09/materialist -feminisms-against-neoliberalism.

Collins, Patricia Hill. 1989. "The Social Construction of Black Feminist Thought." *Signs* 14(4): 745–73. http://www.jstor.org/stable/3174683.

Covington Ward, Yolanda. 2013. "Fighting Phantoms: Mammy, Matriarch, and Other Ghosts Haunting Black Mothers in the Academy." In *Laboring Positions: Black Women, Mothering and the Academy*, ed. Sekile Nzinga-Johnson. Toronto: Demeter Press.

Cox, Aimee. 2008. *Women of Color Faculty at the University of Michigan: Recruitment, Retention, and Campus Climate*. Report prepared for the University of Michigan Center for the Education of Women. http://www.cew .umich.edu/wp-content/uploads/2018/06/AimeeCoxWOCFull2_3.pdf.

duCille, Ann. 1994. "The Occult of True Black Womanhood: Critical Demeanor and Black Feminist Studies." *Signs* 19(3): 591–629. http://www .jstor.org/stable/3174771.

Gill, Rosalind. 2009. "Breaking the Silence: The Hidden Injuries of Neo-liberal Academia." In *Secrecy and Silence in the Research Process: Feminist Reflections*, ed. Roísín Ryan-Flood and Rosalind Gill. London: Routledge.

Harley, Debra A. 2008. "Maids of Academe: African American Women Faculty at Predominately White Institutions." *Journal of African American Studies* 12(1): 19–36. http://www.jstor.org/stable/41819156.

Lorde, Audre. 1980. "Age, Race, Class and Sex: Women Redefining Difference." Paper delivered at the Copeland Colloquium, Amherst College, Amherst, MA. Reproduced in *Sister Outsider*. Trumansburg, NY: Crossing Press, 1984.

McCluskey, Molly. 2017. "Public Universities Get an Education in Private Industry." *Atlantic*, April 3. https://www.theatlantic.com/education /archive/2017/04/public-universities-get-an-education-in-private -industry/521379.

Menges, Robert J., and William H. Exum. 1983/2016. "Barriers to the Progress of Women and Minority Faculty." *Journal of Higher Education* 54(2): 123–44. Published online November 1, 2016.

Mitchell, Michael, Michael Leachman, Kathleen Masterson, and Samantha Waxman. 2018. "Unkept Promises: State Cuts to Higher Education Threaten Access and Equity." Center on Budget and Policy Priorities. https://www.cbpp.org/research/state-budget-and-tax/unkept-promises -state-cuts-to-higher-education-threaten-access-and.

Motta, Sara. 2012. "The Messiness of Motherhood in the Marketised University." Beautiful Transgressions column, *Ceasefire* (June). http:// ceasefiremagazine.co.uk/messiness-motherhood-marketised-university.

Newfield, Christopher. 2011. *Unmaking the Public University: The Forty-Year Assault on the Middle Class*. Cambridge, MA: Harvard University Press.

Nzinga-Johnson, Sekile, ed. 2013. *Laboring Positions: Black Women, Mothering and the Academy*. Toronto: Demeter Press.

Patton, Stacey. 2012. "The PhD Now Comes with Food Stamps." *Chronicle of Higher Education* (May 6). Accessed August 3, 2015. http://chronicle.com /article/From-Graduate-School-to/131795.

Rogers, Juhanna Nicole. 2015. "On the Burdens Carried by Single Black Mothers Enrolled in PhD Programs." For Harriet, March 4. Accessed August 3, 2015. http://www.forharriet.com/2015/03/the-burdens-carried -by-single-black.html#axzz3eTAxxthS.

Shumway, David. 2017. "The University, Neoliberalism, and the Humanities: A History." *Humanities* 6(4): 83. https://doi.org/10.3390/h6040083.

Trower, C. A., and R. P. Chait. 2002. "Faculty Diversity: Too Little for Too Long." *Harvard Magazine* 98 (March–April): 33–37.

Truman Commission on Higher Education. 1947. *Higher Education for Democracy: A Report of the President's Commission on Higher Education*. Vol. 1, *Establishing the Goals*. New York: Harper and Brothers.

Turner, Caroline Sotello Viernes. 2000. "New Faces, New Knowledge." *Academe* 86: 34–38.

———. 2002. "Women of Color in Academe: Living with Multiple Marginal-ity." *Journal of Higher Education* 73(1): 74–93.

Turner, Caroline Sotello Viernes, and Samuel L. Myers. 2000. *Faculty of Color in Academe: Bittersweet Success*. Boston: Allyn and Bacon.

Williams, Rhonda. 2002. "Getting Paid: Black Women Economists Reflect on Black Women and Work." In *Sister Circle: Black Women and Work*, ed. Sharon Harley. New Brunswick, NJ: Rutgers University Press.

Conclusion

Gill, Rosalind. 2009. "Breaking the Silence: The Hidden Injuries of Neo-liberal Academia." In *Secrecy and Silence in the Research Process: Feminist Reflections*, ed. Roísín Ryan-Flood and Rosalind Gill. London: Routledge.

hooks, bell. 1994. *Teaching to Transgress: Education as the Practice of Freedom*. New York: Routledge.

Morrison, Toni. 2015. "No Place for Self-Pity, No Room for Fear." *Nation*, April 6. https://www.thenation.com/article/no-place-self-pity-no-room-fear.

Index